Learn French Handbook for Adult Beginners

Essential French Words And Phrases You Must Know!

Table of Contents

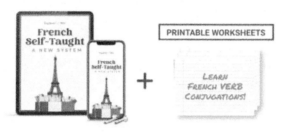

Introduction

It's not just about enjoying the incredible French architecture or tasting the local food when visiting France, connecting with people is what makes each trip memorable.

Nevertheless, learning French can seem like a daunting task that requires more time than you usually have. This is particularly important since the average understanding of English in France isn't as high as it is in other countries.

You might be surprised to learn that you don't need to know too many French words or complete grammar to connect with locals. Most people use just a limited number of words and expressions in a single situation, and many of those are quite repetitive. For example, you will probably not discuss politics, if you are ordering coffee and croissants at a cafe. To help you get by in most everyday situations with the least amount of effort, this book is designed based on a context–based approach.

The book is structured into logical sequences that correspond to actual contextual situations. We carefully covered all possible situations you may encounter as a foreigner traveling around France, assembling the most important words and phrases in a logical, no–frills format. Our carefully chosen phrases are sure to make you feel confident in any given situation. The different sections of the book cover topics such as accommodation, transportation, eating and drinking, shopping, sightseeing, business, visiting a doctor, talking about hobbies and much more.

Additionally, there are sections that explain how to deal with some common problems, such as losing a passport, exchanging an item you bought, or getting lost in a city. Having traveled to foreign countries, as well as you, we understand all the crazy situations one may face.

As language lovers and learners, we have tried many different approaches and have found that internalizing situations works best. What does this mean? Imagine being in a cafe, queuing at the doctor's office or asking for directions. Creating mental images while learning is a method that enhances your memory. Because of the way our brains work, visualizing makes it easier to remember. Images by their nature are quickly recalled. The more vivid the image, the more likely we are to remember it. Our brain is automatically triggered when we see a similar scene, making it easier to recall the dialogues or useful phrases we once learned.

The purpose of this book is not to serve as a complete field guide, but rather as a reference, study, and review resource. At the beginning of the book, you'll get a basic understanding of French pronunciations and accents. You'll also learn one of the most powerful tools when learning any language – the IPA transcription system. IPA transcription is a standardized way to write speech sounds in any language, whether you can read or not. After learning the IPA elements, you'll be able to read French transcription without a single mistake.

At the beginning, you'll also be introduced to basic French grammar just enough for you to understand the most frequent words, such as pronouns, possessive pronouns, verbs and adjectives. You will note that certain structures, such as "I am", and "where is" appear frequently throughout the book. The thing is that the more you practice the essential structures included here, the easier it will be for you to recall the statements once you need them, and even create a phrase of your own.

Additionally, your experience will be enriched by a basic understanding of French etiquette. French are big on politeness, and learning a couple of politeness can take you a long way. Knowing how to address people in France can sometimes be more helpful than correctly asking for help.

In this book you'll get:

→ **IPA Pronunciation Guide** to help you read the French transcription.

→ A detailed **Pronunciation Guide** to pronounce vowels, consonants and learn accents in the French language (including their combinations).

→ **Basic French Grammar Guide** to help you get familiar with the most frequent French words, such as pronouns, articles, adjectives or verbs.

→ **Over 3 000 common phrases in French**, with an accurate translation in English.

→ **Transcription** of each and every word in the phrases, included after every translation.

→ **Social Etiquette Tips**.

Language learners often complain about not having enough material that can help them with everyday conversations. So, even if you are taking French courses, you'll find tons of useful examples and a good companion to your French classes in this book.

Besides being linguists and language enthusiasts, the authors speak French natively, so they know exactly how to apply the language in real life. Additionally, they will also be able to teach you how to speak and sound like a true native, and avoid some bookish expressions no one really uses.

Even if you don't have much time to study, simply carrying the book around will enable you to quickly find the needed French words. Having this book at your fingertips will make it easy for you to connect on a deeper level with French people and culture, and make some really good memories.

Your days founding the right word or response in French are finally over. It's time to picture yourself in France.

How to read IPA transcription

Every aspiring French learner should learn to read the *International Phonetic Alphabet* (IPA) because it's a powerful tool when learning any language. Because most languages are not spelled phonetically, we need help reading the language. IPA stands for International Phonetic Alphabet, which is a standardized alphabet for phonetic notation. Each symbol of the IPA has a unique pronunciation, no matter what language you're learning. You should know there's no one–letter–to–one–symbol correspondence between an IPA transcription and its normal spelling.

For example, the French word "*house*" is written "*maison*" but pronounced [mɛzɔ□], according to IPA standards.

Let's see some more examples:

French spelling / IPA transcription

famille – [famij]

aussi – [osi]

enfin – [ãfɛ̃]

beaucoup – [boku]

Now that you are studying French, you should become familiar with the French sounds. Pay attention that French sounds could be different from French letters. We'll discuss this in the next chapter. The Standard French contains the following sounds:

Consonants – /b/ /d/ /f/ /k/ /l/ /m/ /n/ /p/ /s/ /t/ /v//z/ /g/ /ŋ/ /ʁ/ /ʃ/ /ʒ/ / dʒ // tʃ/

Vowels – /a/ /e/ /ɛ/ /ə/ /i/ /ɔ/ /o/ /œ/ /ø/ /u/ /y/

Semi–vowels – /j/ /w/ /ɥ/

Immediately, you'll see a few sounds that aren't similar to your native language, like /ç/, /œ/ /ø/, so you'll need to take extra care to get them right.

Vowels

IPA / French vowels	French words	English Approximation
a	patte, là, femme	tr**a**p
ɑ	pâte, glas	br**a**
e	clé, les, chez, aller, pied, journée, et	l**ace**
ɛ	baie, faite, mettre, renne, crème, peine, violet	b**e**st
ɛ : (longer)	fête, maître, reine	**fai**ry
ə (known as e silent)	reposer, monsieur	**ag**ain
i	si, île, régie, pays, fils	b**ea**t
œ	sœur, jeune, club	b**ir**d
ø	ceux, jeûner, queue	b**ur**n
o	saut, haut, chose, bureau	st**o**ry

u	coup, roue	sh**oo**t
y	tu, sûr, rue	the sound is non existent in English

Semivowels / Semiconsonants

IPA / French Semivowels	French words	English Approximation
j	payer, fille, travail, hier	**y**oga
w	oui, loi, web	**w**et
ɥ	huit	Hu**ey**

Nasal Vowels

Unlike French, English does not have nasal vowels, so the English approximation here is only a rough guide.

IPA / Nasal vowels	French words	English Approximation
ɑ̃	sans, champ, temps, vent, Jean, taon	roughly like s**ong**, but more nasalized

ɛ̃	vin, pain, plein, bien, impair, Reims, synthèse, sympathique	roughly like h**ang**, but more nasalized
œ̃	un, parfum	roughly like b**urn**, but more nasalized
ɔ̃	son, nom	roughly like dr**awn**, but more nasalized

Consonants

IPA / French consonants	French words	English Approximation
b	bon	a**b**out
d	deux, grande	to**d**ay
f	faire, vif	**f**estival
g	garçon, longue	a**g**ain
k	corps, avec	s**k**y
l	laver, seul	**l**evel
m	mère	**m**other

n	nous, bonne	no
ɲ	gagner, champagne	canyon
p	père, groupe	spy
ʁ	regarder, nôtre	Guttural R, non existent in English
s	sans, ça, assez	sir
ʃ	chance	shoe
t	thé, tout	sty
v	vous, wagon, neuf heures, vous	vein
z	zéro, raison, chose	zero
ʒ	jamais, visage	measure

Chapter 1: French Pronunciation and Alphabet

Avoir une autre langue, c'est posséder une deuxième âme.

Charlemagne

French uses the same 26 letters as the English alphabet. However, as you might expect, it has a different pronunciation.

These are (*a, b, c, d, e, f, g, h, i, j, k, l, m, n, o, p, q, r, s, t, u, v, w, x, y, z*).

Even though some French letters look like English letters, don't assume they are pronounced the same. It is the case with letters "j" and "g", which are proving to be a stumbling block for many French students.

While the French language has 26 letters of the alphabet, it also contains 36 sounds (phonemes), much more than the letters.

Sounds are grouped into three categories:

- vowels

- semivowels

- consonants

In some cases (well, in many cases), the pronunciation depends on the sounds surrounding it. In the following chapter, you'll be explained how vowels, semivowels, nasal vowels and consonants sound in

French, and how their pronunciation changes when combined with different letters.

Vowels

There are six vowels in the French language (a, e, i, o, u, y). Sometimes, they can be written with accents. It is important to note that they do not always sound the same as in English. Combined with other vowels or consonants, they can create a completely different sound.

Vowel – A

"A" is usually pronounced like the "a" in the English word "flat", but it requires widening the corners of the mouth. In other cases, it can be pronounced like "ah" in the word "father", especially if it contains the circumflex or the grave accent.

Don't worry if you see variants of "a" with a diacritical mark (**A, À , Â**), because in all these cases the "a" is pronounced similarly.

Vowel – E

"E" can be pronounced in many ways, depending on the accent. When it is found at the end of the word, it remains silent. Like in these examples:

- petite (small) /pətitə/
- lourde (heavy) /luʀd/

The sound "e" has a variety of different spellings.

- **Without an accent**, it is often called silent "e", and it is pronounced like "oo" in the English word "look", denoted by "uh".
- petite (small) /pətitə/
- **É** (with an acute accent)

Position your tongue like you're about to say "ay", but once you start making noise, don't move your tongue or lips. Keep them steady for the entire duration of the sound.

- été (summer) /ete/

- café (coffee) /kafe/

- **È, Ê, and Ë** (with a grave, circumflex or diaeresis mark)

It's pronounced like the "e" in the English word error, only flatter.

- très (very) /tʀe/

- rêve (dream) /ʀɛve/

- père (father) /pɛʀe/

Vowel – I

It's pronounced similarly to "ee" in the English word "meet". Orthographically, it can be written in several ways, always using one letter (**i, î, y**), except for some words that are borrowed from English. In this case, a digraph (two letters) is used to express the sound "i".

It happens with the letters **–ea** and **–ee**, like in English borrowed words such as *jean, leader, cheeseburger, feeling, meeting.*

- rire (to laugh) /ʀiʀə/

- corriger (to correct) /kɔʀiʒe/

Vowel – O

It's pronounced like the "o" in the English word "cold". However, the sound "o" has a variety of possible spellings (o, ô, au, eau).

- **O**

- abricot (apricot) /abʀiko/

- dos (back) /do/

- **Ô**

- poser (to put down) /poze/
- diplôme (diploma certificate) /diplomə/
- **AU**
- épaule (shoulder) /epolə/
- jaune (yellow) /ʒon/
- **EAU**
- bateau (boat) /bato/
- château (castle) /ʃato/

Vowel – U

The closest sound to "u" in English is the word "soup" or "boot". All variants of the sound "u" are pronounced the same way (*ou, où, oû, aoû*).

- oublier (to forget) /ublije/
- coûter (to cost) /kute/

Vowel – Y

It may be challenging to pronounce "Y" because the sound does not exist in English. A similar sound is "oo" as in "food," but in French, the lips are much more rounded. When producing the French "Y" sound, lips should make a small hole, while the tongue takes the same position as when pronouncing "i" , with the tongue slightly bent down touching the lower teeth.

The pronunciation of "y" is unaffected by accents. So, whether it's spelled "u" or "*û*", the pronunciation remains the same.

- sucre (sugar) /sykʀə/
- tu (you) /ty/
- bûche (log) /byʃə/

Semi vowels / Semi consonants

In French, there are 3 semivowels, which are also called transitive sounds. All three (**u, y, i**) are formed when they come into contact with another vowel.

U + vowel / **w**

Y + vowel / **ɥ**

I + vowel / **j**

[w]

The [w] sounds like the letter "w" in English. A relaxed "wuh" followed by a quick "ah" sound. It sound similar to the beginning of the word *watch* /watʃ/ in English.

oi + vowel

louer (to rent) /lwe/

oe + vowel

foi (faith) /fwa/

ou + vowel

moelle (marrow) /mwal/

[ɥ]

It uses about the same lip position as the [w] semivowel. However, instead of keeping your tongue relaxed, your tongue should be tight against your hard palate.

u + i

cuire (to cook) /kɥiʀə/

u + some other vowel

juin (june) /ʒɥɛ□/

[j]

13

Known as the "yod" in French, due to the "yuh" sound, it's often spelled with a "y." A "yuh" sound in the initial position, followed by various vowels. The initial sound is similar to that of yoga, yellow, and yes in English.

i + vowel

bien (well, good) /bjɛ□/

y + vowel

yaourt (yogurt) /jauʀt/

−ill

abeille (bee) /abɛjə/

−ail

détail (detail) /detaj/

−eil

appareil (device) /apaʀɛj/

−ouil

soleil (sun) /sɔlɛj/

−euil

deuil (mourning, grief) /dœj/

Nasal Vowels

The French language is known for its nasal sounds that do not have any equivalent in English. There are two types of vowels in French: oral vowels (pronounced by passing air through the mouth) and nasal vowels (pronounced by passing air through the nose and the mouth, instead of just through the mouth).

Nasal sounds are vowels followed by an "n" or an "m". There are three nasal vowels used in French (nasal a, nasal i, and nasal o).

- ã – **nasal a** (pronounced like a nasalized "aun" in the word "laundry").

- ɛ̃ – **nasal i** (pronounced like a nasalized "an" in the word "angle").

- ɔ̃ – **nasal o** (pronounced like a nasalized "on" in the words "balloon" or "shadow").

Here's a table where you can find what the spelling looks like for each of the nasal vowels.

ã – nasal a	ɛ̃ – nasal i	ɔ̃ – nasal o
Spelling **AN, AM, EM, EN**	Spelling **IN, IM, AIN, AIM, EIN, EIM, UN, UM, EN, EM final EN**	Spelling **ON, OM**
– grand (tall) /gʀã/ – blanc (white) /blã/ – ambiance (atmosphere) /ãbjãs/ – temps (weather) /tã/ – enfant (child) /ãfã/	– intéresser (to interest) /ɛ̃teʀəse/ – pain (bread) /pɛ̃/ – faim (hunger) /fɛ̃/ – imposer (to impose) /ɛ̃poze/ – Reims (city in France) /ʀɛ̃s/ – chien (dog) /ʃjɛ̃/ – thym (thym) /tɛ̃/	– bon (good) /bɔ̃/ – ombre (shadow) /ɔ̃bʀ/

However, it doesn't mean that all vowels followed by "n" or "m" make a nasal sound. French students often have trouble distinguishing between the two cases, even though the rule is simple. There are two situations in which nasal vowels aren't pronounced nasally. When the diphthong or triphthong is followed by another vowel or, when the consonant is doubled. Let's see some examples where the nasal sound isn't pronounced.

1. Followed by a vowel

aimer (to love) /eme/

vanille (vanilla) /vanij/

omettre (to left out) /ɔmɛtʀ/

2. Double Consonant

immeuble (building) /imœbl/

homme (man) /ɔm/

Consonants

In French, the most challenging part is the vowels. Having mastered those, consonants become pretty straightforward, because most consonants are pronounced like in English. Except for a few of them.

Consonants that remain the same as in English are: **b, c, d, f, g, k, l, m, n, p, s, t, v, w, x, y** and **z**.

Let's take a look at the ones that are different.

French consonants	Pronunciation	Examples
h	Always silent.	heureux (happy) /ørø/ homme (man) /ɔm/
j	Sounds like –s in the English word "television".	jupe (skirt) /ʒyp/ jaune (yellow) /ʒon/
q/que	Sounds like the letter –c, and –k in the English words "cat" and "kettle".	cinq (five) /sɛ̃k/ quatre (four) /katʀ/
r, rr	Nonexistent in the English language. It sounds like a gargling sound.	rose (pink) /ʀoz/ radis (radish) /ʀadi/

In French, when followed by certain vowels, some consonants make different sounds to English.

Consonants followed by vowels	Pronunciation	Examples
c + e, i, y	–s	cinéma (cinema) /sinema/ glace (ice) /glas/ garçon (boy) /gaʀsɔ̃/
g + e, i, y	Makes a sound like "s" in "television".	girafe (girafe) /ʒiʀaf/ singe (monkey) /sɛ̃ʒ/

s between vowels	−z	rose (rose) /roz/ maison (house) /mɛzɔ̃/ chemise (shirt) /ʃ(ə)miz/

Double consonants

When placed next to another consonant, some consonants make a different sound to English.

Double Consonants	Pronunciation	Examples
ch	−sh	chat (cat) /ˈtʃæt/ cheval (horse) /ʃ(ə)val/
th	−t	thé (tea) /te/
gn	−n, followed by "y" like in the English word "onion".	mignon (cute) /miɲɔ̃/
i + ll	English "y" sound.	famille (family) /famij/

In the case the same consonant is doubled, its pronunciation is not altered.

Silent consonants

The majority of consonants at the end of the words are not pronounced in French. These letters are referred to as silent letters. Letters *d*, *p*, *s*, *t*, *x*, *z* are silent at the end of a word, like in these examples:

- Beaucoup (a lot) /boku/
- Heureux (happy) /øRø/
- Hommes (men) /ɔm/
- Pot (jar) /po/

However, the letters *c*, *r* and *f* can sometimes be pronounced. These letters require extra attention.

- Sac (bag) /sak/
- Neuf (new) /nœf/
- Jour (day) /ʒuR/

Liaisons

The French language can sound incomprehensible at times, because of a particular French characteristic that is called "*liaison*". "*Liaison*" means that two words or even an entire sentence can sound like one word. This happens when the end of one word is linked to the next word by sounding the silent letter. The letters *d*, *n*, *s*, *t*, *x* and *z* that are normally silent, can be sounded when the next word starts with a vowel or a *h* and this is what we call "*liaison*".

Pay attention that sounds **S** and **X** will sound like **Z** when they are followed by a vowel.

Let's see some examples:

- C'est un ami. (liaison in T between "est" and "un", and liaison in N between "un" and "ami").
- Nous avons. (liaison in Z between "nous" and "avons").

- Deux heures. (liaison in Z between "deux" and "heures").

Stress

Tonic accents in French are quite different from those in English. There is one stressed syllable in every English word, meaning that one syllable is pronounced more emphatically than the others.

In French, however, each syllable of a word is pronounced the same way, except for the final syllable of each rhythmic group (sentence).

Take a look at the place of stressed syllables in French and English. While the stress in English often changes place, it is fixed in French.

English – French

- phot**o**graphy – photograph**ie**
- edu**ca**tion – éduca**tion**
- **re**giment – régi**ment**

Whenever there is a whole sentence in French, the stress is transferred to the last syllable. Pay attention to how the stress moves with each word added.

- Je visite la cathé**drale**.
- Je visite la cathédrale Notre **Dame.**
- Je visite la cathédrale Notre Dame à P**aris**.

Accent

There are five different kinds of accent marks used in written French. They are:

acute accent (*accent aigu*)	grave accent (*accent grave*)	circumflex (*accent circonflexe*)	diaeresis (*tréma*)	cedilla (*cédille*)
é only	è, à, ù	â, ê, î, ô, û	ë, ï, ü, ÿ	ç only

Chapter 2: Basic French Grammar

Une langue différente est une vision différente de la vie.

Federico Fellini

Articles

The French language is one of the languages where nouns have two genders: masculine and feminine. Although there are some rules for determining whether a noun is masculine or feminine, the truth is that most of the time, you have to learn it by heart.

Articles help you determine the gender of the noun, as they stand in front of each of them. All nouns in French are either **masculine, feminine** and **singular** or **plural**.

The French language distinguishes between definite and indefinite articles.

Indefinite Articles

An indefinite article indicates an unspecified or unidentified noun. French has three types of indefinite articles, equivalent to the English "a/an" and "some".

Masculine Singular	Feminine Singular	Plural (masculine and feminine)
UN (un homme, un chien)	**UNE** (une femme, une maison)	**DES** (des maisons, des hommes, des femmes)

It is sometimes possible to choose (some, any) or even leave out a word when translating articles from French to English.

J'ai des amis formidables. – I have (some) great friends.

You don't need an article if you are talking about a person's profession, religion or in negative sentences.

Je suis étudiant en français. – I am a French student.

Je ne veux pas de chien. – I don't want a dog.

*Note that the French word **un** is both a number and an indefinite article for masculine nouns.

Definite Articles

It is also common in French to use the definite article to refer to general concepts. There is only one definite article in English: **the**. As opposed to French which has four of them (*le, la, l', les*).

Sometimes, English speakers find it challenging to add a word that is not needed in English. Try adding "generally" to the end of your sentence, and if it works, use the definite article.

Masculine Singular	Feminine Singular	Plural (masculine and feminine)
LE (l') (l'homme, le chien)	**LA (l')** (la femme, la maison)	**LES** (les maisons, les hommes, les femmes)

Nouns

Plural Nouns

To create the plural form of a noun, you have to:

- change the article to *les/des*.
- make a plural noun, according to the rules.

In general, a plural noun is formed by adding **–s**, and that –s is almost never spoken.

Singular – le billet / Plural – les billets

Singular – un billet / Plural – des billets

Apart from the general rule, in almost all other cases (when a noun ends in –eau, –au, –eu, –ou, –al, –ail) you should add **–x.**

un château – des châteaux

un cheveu – des cheveux

un genou – des genoux

un journal – des journaux

un vitrail – des vitraux

Feminine Form

As you learned, French differentiates masculine and feminine genres. This is how to form a feminine genre out of masculine.

Forming feminine form	Examples
Add **−e** to the masculine form.	*un ami => une amie (a friend)*
Change the ending **−er** to **−ère**.	*l'écolier => l'écolière (the student)*
Change the ending **−eur** to **−euse**.	*un voleur => une voleuse (a thief)*
Change the ending **−teur** to **−trice**.	*un directeur => une directrice (a director)*

Pronouns

One of the most frequent words you'll see in this guide are pronouns. They replace people, places, and things which have already been mentioned. They also reflect grammatical gender, person, and number.

Depending on its role in a sentence, a pronoun can be either the subject or the object of the sentence. In French, for each function in a sentence (subject, direct object, indirect object), the pronouns have different forms, as you can see in this table.

Personal Pronouns

Personal Pronouns (Subject Pronouns in weak form)	Subject Pronoun/ (strong form – used only without a verb)	Direct Object Pronouns	Indirect Object Pronouns
Je/J' – I	**Moi** – I	**Me/m'** – me	**Me/m'** – Me
Tu – you	**Toi** – You	**Te/t'** – you	**Te/t'** – You
Il – he **Elle** – she	**Lui** – He **Elle** – She	**Le/l'** – him, it **La/l'** – her, it	**Lui** – Him (it) **Lui** – Her (it)
Nous – We	**Nous** – We	**Nous** – Us	**Nous** – Us
Vous – You	**Vous** – You	**Vous** – You	**Vous** – You
Ils – They **Elles** – They	**Eux** – They **Elles** – They	**Les** – Them	**Leur** – Them

You choose the correct pronoun according to the noun you want to replace. Keep in mind whether the noun is masculine, feminine, singular or plural, and its grammatical value (is it subject, direct object, indirect object).

*J'ai une copine. **Elle** est très gentille et je **l**'aime beaucoup.* – I have a friend. She is very kind and I like her a lot.

(**J'** – subject pronoun, **elle** – subject pronoun, **l'** – direct object pronoun).

For example, "elle" is used to replace a feminine singular noun, serving as the subject, while "l'" refers to "copine" too, but serves as a direct object.

Subject pronouns refer to who/what is performing the action.

<u>J'</u>ai une copine. <u>**Elle**</u> est très gentille. – I have a friend. She is very kind. (weak subject form used always with the verb).

Qui chante des chansons ? – **Moi**. – Who sings songs? – Me. (strong subject form, used without a verb, and to emphasize).

Lui, il est trop gentil. / He, he is so kind. (strong subject form).

Object Pronouns refers to who/what is the direct receiver of the action. There are two types of object pronouns, according to the attachment type with the verb.

→ **Direct object pronoun** replaces a noun that comes directly after a verb without a preposition. "*Acheter un livre*" is a direct relation between a verb and an object.

J'ai acheté le livre. Je l'ai acheté. – I bought the book. I bought it.

(Je – personal pronoun, l' (it) – direct object pronoun, referring to "the book").

→ **Indirect object pronoun** replaces a noun as well as the preposition *à/de*, which introduces the indirect object. "*Chanter à*" is an example of indirect object relation.

J'ai chanté des chansons à ma copine. Je <u>lui</u> ai chanté des chansons. – I sang songs to my friend. I sang songs to her.

Adjectives

Descriptive Adjectives

The French adjectives present a bit more difficulty than the English ones. The reason is that French adjectives need to agree with the word they describe, in gender (masculine and feminine) and number (singular and plural). In fact, in French, all words in a sentence must agree with each other: verbs agree with the subject, adjectives agree with the noun or pronoun and so on.

Take the basic form of an adjective (which is always masculine) and add −**e** to create a feminine form. It's important to note that adding this −**e** causes the formerly silent consonant to be pronounced.

Singular m. – *un **grand** garçon* Singular f. – *une **grande** fille*

Plural m. – *des **grands** garçons* Singular f. – *des **grandes** filles*

As you may noticed, one English word "tall" has 4 different variants in French to express:

- **Singular masculin**
- **Singular feminine** / add −**e**
- **Plural masculin** / add −**s**
- **Plural feminine** / add −**es**

Be careful when you spot masculine adjectives ending in −**e** (add −e), −**eux** (change to −**euse**), −**f** (change to −**ve**), −**er** (change to −**ère**), ending in consonants (double the final consonant).

âgé – âgée / dangereux – dangereuse /neuf – neuve / cher – chère / bon – bonne

Possessive Adjectives

Possessive adjectives are used to express ownership. Compared to English, French has a few differences, so let's take a look.

my book – **mon** livre

my house – **ma** maison

my books – **mes** livres

As you can notice, the English possessive adjective "my" has three variations in French (masculine, feminine and plural). That's why French has 18 possessive adjectives, while English has only 7.

Depending on the noun they describe, **French possessive adjectives** take different forms. In other words, if the noun is masculine and singular, the possessive adjective should be too.

The **masculine singular possessive adjectives** are: *mon, ton, son, notre, votre, leur.*

The **feminine singular possessive adjectives** are: *ma, ta, sa, notre, votre, leur.*

The **plural possessive adjectives** are the same for both genders: *mes, tes, ses, nos, vos, leurs.*

Personal Pronouns	Masculine Singular	Feminine Singular	Masculine/Feminine Plural (plural owners and plural possessions)
Je	**Mon** – my	**Ma** – my	**Mes** – my
Tu	**Ton** – your	**Ta** – your	**Tes** – yours
Il/Elle/On	**Son** – his/her	**Sa** – his/her	**Ses** – his/her
Nous	**Notre** – our	**Notre** – our	**Nos** – our

Vous	**Votre** – your	**Votre** – your	**Vos** – your
Ils/Elles	**Leur** – their	**Leur** – their	**Leurs** – their

While in English the gender of an owner is obvious, in French it's impossible to determine whether the owner is masculine or feminine. Instead, we are considering the genre of a thing owned, which is not the case in English. **"Son chapeau"** shows that the word *"chapeau"* is masculine. In English, it can be translated as either **"his** hat" or **"her** hat".

Verbs and Tenses

French has 10 indicative tenses, but not all of them are used in everyday language. For day to day conversations, you'll need the basic ones such as:

→ *le présent* (the present)

→ *le passé composé* (the simple past)

→ *l'imparfait* (the imperfect)

→ *le futur proche* (the near future)

→ *le futur simple* (the future simple)

French Conjugation

The French conjugation system is quite complex. All French verbs must be conjugated in person and number, which ends in having six different forms of each verb. Learning French conjugations involves learning which verbs are regular and which aren't. To distinguish regular from irregular verbs, French has classified all verbs into three categories known as groups in French. There are 3 groups and you'll easily recognize which verbs fall into which category by looking at their endings.

- **I group** – regular verbs whose infinitive ends in –**ER**.
- **II group** – regular verbs with an infinitive ending in –**IR**.
- **III group** – irregular verbs.

Present Tense

It is easier to use French present tense than English present tense for one reason. We have four forms of the present tense in English: the Present Simple, the Present Perfect, the Present Continuous, and the Present Perfect Continuous, while there's only one in French. French Present is used to express momentary action as well as progressive action.

The present tense in French (*le présent*) is used to talk about:

- facts that are always true.
- current situations.
- habits and repeated actions.
- scheduled future actions.

To express *Present Progressive and Present Perfect*, French uses expressions.

→ **Expressing Present Progressive in French** – use the expression "*être en train de*" or literally, "to be in the process of."

Je suis en train de lire. – I am reading.

Elle est en train de finir la course. – She's finishing the race.

→ Expressing Present Perfect – use depuis + présent de l'indicatif, which means since, for actions that began in the past and continue into the present.

J'habite à Paris depuis un an. – I've lived in Paris for a year.

J'étudie le français depuis deux ans. – I've studied French for two years (and still do).

Regular Verbs

Regular –**ER** and –**IR** verbs are conjugated the same way in all tenses and moods.

I GROUP ER – Remove the infinitive ending –**ER** and then add one of the following verb endings: –**e**, –**es**, –**e**, –**ons**, –**ez**, –**ent**.

II Group IR – Remove the infinitive ending –**IR**, and add different endings: –**is**, –**is**, –**it**, –**issons**, –**issez**, –**issent**.

Personal Pronouns	I GROUP / –RE endings	*Parler* (–RE verb)	II GROUP / –IR endings	*Finir* (–IR verb)
Je	–**e**	Parl**e** – I speak	–**is**	Fin**is** – I finish
Tu	–**es**	Parl**es** – You speak	–**is**	Fin**is** – You finish
Il/Elle/On	–**e**	Parl**e** – He/she speaks	–**it**	Fin**it** – He/She finishes
Nous	–**ons**	Parl**ons** – We speak	–**issons**	Fin**issons** – We finish

| Vous | −ez | Parlez − You speak | −issez | Finissez − You finish |
| Ils/Elles | −ent | Parlent − They speak | −issent | Finissent − They finish |

*Not every verb ending in −**er** is regular. You should always be aware of exceptions. For instance, the most common verb ***aller*** (to go) is irregular.

Irregular Verbs

Here are the most common irregular verbs in French.

	Être − to be	*Avoir* − to have	*Faire* − to do	*Aller* − to go	*Boire* − to drink	*Savoir* − to know
Je	suis	ai	fais	vais	bois	sais
Tu	es	as	fais	vas	bois	sais
Il/Elle/On	est	a	fait	va	boit	sait
Nous	sommes	avons	faisons	allons	buvons	savons
Vous	êtes	avez	faites	allez	buvez	savez
Ils/Elles	sont	ont	font	vont	boivent	savent

	Prendre – to take	*Comprendre* – to understand	*Attendre* – to wait	*Pouvoir* – can	*Venir* – to come
Je	prend**s**	comprend**s**	attend**s**	peux	viens
Tu	prend**s**	comprend**s**	attend**s**	peux	viens
Il/Elle/On	prend	comprend	attend	peut	vient
Nous	pren**ons**	compren**ons**	attend**ons**	pouvons	venons
Vous	pren**ez**	compren**ez**	attend**ez**	pouvez	venez
Ils/Elles	pren**nent**	comprenn**ent**	attend**ent**	peuvent	vienn**ent**

Future Tenses

Future Simple

In English, the simple future is analogous to the "will" form.

The future simple is used in the following cases:

- **when talking about future intentions.**

Demain j'étudierai la grammaire. – Tomorrow I will study grammar.

- **when making suppositions or predictions about the future.**

Tu n'arriveras jamais à l'heure. – You will never arrive on time.

- **in conditional sentences.**

Si on attend les soldes, on paiera moins. – If we wait for the sales, we will pay less.

Regular Verbs

To form the future simple with regular verbs, just take the infinitive form and add the future endings: *–ai, –as, –a, –ons, –ez* and *–ont*. Take the infinitive form for **–ER** and **–IR** verbs, but remove final **–E** for regular **–RE** verbs, before adding endings.

Personal Pronouns	I Group – ER	II Group – IR	III Group –RE drop the –e + add endings
Je	aimer+**ai**	finir+**ai**	Prendr<u>e</u> / prendr +**ai**
Tu	aimer+**as**	finir+**as**	prendr+**as**
Il/Elle	aimer+**a**	finir+**a**	prendr+**a**
Nous	aimer+**ons**	finir+**ons**	prendr+**ons**
Vous	aimer+**ez**	finir+**ez**	prendr+**ez**
Ils/Elles	aimer+**ont**	finir+**ont**	prendr+**ont**

Irregular Verbs

Most frequent verbs are actually irregular in the future.

- aller → **ir** → j'**irai** / *I will go*
- avoir → **aur** → j'**aurai** / *I will have*
- être → **ser** → je **serai** / *I will be*
- faire → **fer** → je **ferai** / *I will do*
- pouvoir → **pourr** → je **pourrai** / *l will be able*
- devoir → **devr** → je **devrai** / *I will need*
- savoir → **saur** → je **saurai** / *I will know*
- venir → **viendr** → je **viendrai** / *I will come*
- voir → **verr** → je **verrai** / *I will see*
- vouloir → **voudr** → je **voudrai** / *I will want*
- envoyer → **enverr** → j'enverrai / *I will send*

Futur Proche

"*Futur proche*" refers to near future actions. This is equivalent to the English structure ***going to*** + **infinitive**, implying an intent behind the action. The *Futur proche* is used when an action shortly takes place or for planned actions in the future.

Christine va partir dans deux secondes. – Christina is leaving in two seconds.

Il va aller au supermarché. – He is going to the supermarket.

To conjugate the *futur proche*, we use the present tense of the verb ***aller*** + **verb in infinitive**.

Je	Je **vais + infinitive** (finir, porter, lire)
Tu	Tu **vas + infinitive** (finir, porter, lire)
Il/Elle	Il/Elle **va + infinitive** (finir, porter, lire)
Nous	Nous **allons + infinitive** (finir, porter, lire)
Vous	Vous **allez + infinitive** (finir, porter, lire)
Ils/Elles	Ils/Elles **vont + infinitive** (finir, porter, lire)

Past Tense

In French "*le passé composé*" corresponds to two different English past tenses: the Past Simple Tense and the Present Perfect. It's used to talk about completed actions in the past, and also to emphasize the results or consequences in the present.

We form the *passé composé* using the auxiliary verbs "*avoir*" or "*être*" followed by the past participle *(le participe passé)* of the verb. Auxiliaries are helping verbs, like "to be" and "to do" in English.

passé composé = auxiliary (avoir or être) + past participle.

Elle a fait un gâteau. – She made a cake.

The past participle usually needs to be learnt by heart. It corresponds to English verbs ending in –ed or –en. The French past participle usually ends in –*é*, –*i*, or –*u*.

Auxiliary Verbs

Some verbs go with "*avoir*" and others with "*être*". Most of them construct the *passé composé* with *avoir,* except for movement, state and pronominal verbs.

Verbs that require the auxiliary "*être*":

→ Verbs of movement

aller, entrer, sortir, partir, arriver, monter, descendre, tomber, passer (to go, to go in, to go out, to leave, to arrive, to go up, to go down, to fall down, to spend).

→ Verbs of state

naître, mourir, devenir (to be born, to die, to become).

→ Pronominal Verbs

Verbs accompanied by a reflexive pronoun.

se laver, se lever, se baigner, se peigner, se souvenir (to wash, to get up, to swim, to comb, to remember).

Conjugation with auxiliary "*être*"

- *Je suis entré* (*entrée* – feminine singular) – I entered.
- *Tu es entré* (*entrée* – feminine singular) – You entered.
- *Il est entré. / Elle est entrée.* (*entrée* – feminine singular) – He/She entered.
- *Nous sommes entrés* (*entrées* – feminine plural) – We entered.
- *Vous êtes entrés* (*entrées* – feminine plural) – You entered.
- *Ils sont entrés. / Elles sont entrées.* – They entered.

Conjugation with auxiliary "*avoir*"

- *J'ai fini.* – I finished.
- *Tu as fini.* – You finished.
- *Il a fini / Elle a fini.* – He/She finished.

- *Nous avons fini.* – We finished.
- *Vous avez fini.* – You finished.
- *Ils ont fini / Elles ont fini.* – They finished.

Negative Sentence

In French, a negative sentence is created by writing "*ne* + verb + *pas*". In front of verbs that start with a vowel, use "*n'*".

Je parle français. – Je ne parle pas français.

J'aime le thé. – Je n'aime pas le thé.

In spoken French, the "ne" tends to glide or even disappear. Sometimes, only the "pas" will be pronounced. So train your brain to catch it.

Qui veut de la soupe ? Pas moi ! – Who wants the soup? Not me!

Pas vraiment. – Not really.

Pas si vite. – Not so fast.

Prepositions

Prepositions of Time

→ **Avant** – before

→ **Après** – after

Je te retrouve après/avant le dîner. – I'll meet up with you after/before diner.

→ **Vers** – towards

Je vais vers la gare. – I am going towards the train station.

→ **Depuis** – since

Il habite à Paris depuis 2020. – He's been living in Paris since 2020.

→ **Pendant** – for, during

J'ai étudié le français pendant trois ans. – I studied French for 3 years.

→ **Pour** – for, in order to

C'est un cadeau pour toi. – It's a present for you.

Prepositions of Place and Movement

→ **À** – to (at, in, to)

Aller à la campagne – To go to the countryside.

Ce livre est à Marie. – This book is Marie's.

L'homme aux yeux bleus – The man with blue eyes.

Visites de 11 heures à 13 heures – Visits from 11 to 13 o'clock.

→ **Chez** – at, among

Je te verrai plus tard chez moi, non ? – I'll see you later at my place, right?

→ **Dans** – in, on

Il est dans sa chambre. – He's in his bedroom.

Dans 2 mois – in 2 months.

→ **De** – from

Le toit de la maison – the roof of the house

La voiture de Paul – Paul's car

De Londres à Paris – from London to Paris

Il vient de Londres. – He comes from London.

→ **Derrière** – behind

La porte de derrière – the back door

→ **Devant** – in front of

Il était assis devant moi. – He was sitting in front of me.

→ **En** – in, to, made

J'habite en France. – I live in France.

La mariée est en blanc. – The bride is in white.

Je le verrai en mai. – I'll see him in May.

C'est en verre. – It's made of glass.

→ **En face de** – in front of

Le bus s'arrête en face de chez moi. – The bus stops in front of my house.

→ **Loin de** – far from

La gare n'est pas très loin d'ici. – The station isn't very far from here.

→ **Parmi** – among

Ils étaient parmi les meilleurs de la classe. – They were among the best in the class.

→ **Sous** – under

Sous la pluie – Under the rain

→ **Sur** – on

Pose–le sur la table. – Put it down on the table.

Vous verrez la boulangerie sur votre droite. – You'll see the bakery on your right.

Chapter 3: Basic Vocabulary

Investir dans les voyages, c'est investir en soi–même.

Matthew Karsten

English and French Cognates

If reading most of these words feels like *"déjà vu"*, it only indicates that your English is quite good, if not native. Words like *(location, adresse, profession, téléphone, entrepreneur, calendaire, dentiste, restaurant, pharmacie, page, fête, histoire, menu, omelette, fruit, orange, intelligent)* are called cognates.

You may feel surprised but approximately 1,500 English words derived from French are cognates – exactly the same in both languages. Words ending in **–ion, –al, able, –ible, –ance, –ence, –ent, –ct** often have the same meaning in French and English. Be aware, however, that French pronunciation is almost always different.

- **action** /aksjɔ̃/
- **ambition** /ãbisjɔ̃/
- **attention** /atãsjɔ̃/
- **célébration** /selebʀasjɔ̃/
- **communication** /kɔmynikasjɔ̃/
- **génération** /ʒeneʀasjɔ̃/
- **animal** /animal/
- **capable** /kapabl/
- **ambulance** /ãbylãs/
- **inaccessible** /inaksesibl/
- **objet** /ɔbʒɛ/
- **insecte** /ɛ̃sɛkt/

- **silence** /silãs/
- **indépendance** /ɪndɪˈpɛndəns/
- **correct** /kəˈrɛkt/
- **parfait** /paʀfɛ/

In English, many words ending in **–ical** have French equivalents ending in **–ique**:

- analytical – **analytique** /analitik/
- critical – **critique** /kʀitik/
- logical – **logique** /lɔʒik/

Many adverbs that end in **–ly** in English have an equivalent in French ending in **–ment**:

- absolutely – **absolument** /apsɔlymã/
- correctly – **correctement** /kɔʀɛktəmã/
- directly – **directement** /diʀɛktəmã/
  especially – **spécialement** /spesjalmã/

Many words ending in **–ary** in English have their French equivalent as **–aire**:

- dictionary – **dictionnaire** /diksjɔnɛʀ/
- anniversary – **anniversaire** /anivɛʀsɛʀ/
- necessary – **néccessaire** /nesesɛʀ/
- contrary – **contraire** /kɔ☐tʀɛʀ/
- vocabulary – **vocabulaire** /vɔkabylɛʀ/

Qualities

proche /pʀɔʃ/ – close	**lointain** /lwɛ□tɛ□/ – far
jeune /ʒœn/ – young	**vieux** /vjø/ – old
vrai /vʀɛ/ – true	**faux** /fo/ – false
fort /fɔʀ/ – strong	**faible** /fɛbl/ – weak
doux /du/ – soft	**dur** /dyʀ/ – hard
grand /gʀɑ□/ – big	**petit** /p(ə)ti/ – small
haut /o/ – high	**bas** /bɑ/ – low
puissant /pɥisɑ□/ – strong, powerful	**faible** /fɛbl/ – weak
chaud /ʃo/ – warm	**froid** /fʀwa/ – cold
joyeux /ʒwajø/ – joyful	**triste** /tʀist/ – sad
vrai /vʀɛ/ – true	**faux** /fo/ – fake, untrue
rapide /ʀapid/ – fast	**lent** /lɑ□/ – slow
tôt /to/ – early	**tard** /taʀ/ – late

Colors

As colors are adjectives, they must match the noun in gender and number. However, some colors come with only masculine forms such as *rouge, orange* or *jaune*, while others have both masculine and feminine.

rouge /ʀuʒ/ – red

orange /ɔʀãʒ/ – orange

jaune /ʒon/ – yellow

vert (m.) /vɛʀ/, verte /vɛʀt/ (f.) – green

bleu (m.) /blø/, bleue (f.) /blø/ – blue

violet (m.) /vjɔlɛ/, violette (f.) /vjɔlɛt/ – purple

Blanc (m.) /blã/, blanche (f.) /blãʃ/ – white

noir (m.) /nwar/, noire (f.) /nwar/ – black

gris (m.) /gʀi/, grise (f.) /gʀiz/ – gray

marron /maʀɔ̃/ – brown

rose /ʀoz/– pink

bleu clair /blø klɛʀ/ – light blue

Example:

C'est un chapeau vert. /sɛtan ʃapo vɛʀ/ – It's a green hat.

C'est une robe blanche. /sɛt yn ʀɔb blãʃ/ – It's a white dress.

Cardinal Numbers

It is very important to master the numbers 1–20 because you will see these numbers repeatedly. The number one, actually has two variants (masculine and feminine) while representing an undefined article at the same time.

0 – zéro /zero/

1 – un /ɛ̃/ or **une** /yn/

2 – deux /dø/

3 – trois /trwa/

4 – quatre /katr/

5 – cinq /sɛ̃k/

6 – six /sis/

7 – sept /sɛt/

8 – huit /ɥi(t)/

9 – neuf /nœf/

10 – dix /dis/

11 – onze /ɔ̃z/

12 – douze /duz/

13 – treize /tʀɛz/

14 – quatorze /katɔʀz/

15 – quinze /kɛ̃z/

16 – seize /sɛz/

17 – dix–sept /di(s)sɛt/

18 – dix–huit /dizɥit/

19 – dix–neuf /diznœf/

20 – vingt /vɛ̃/

It's easy to see that the numbers 17, 18, and 19 are simple math problems:

17 = 10 + 7, dix–sept

18 = 10 + 8, dix–huit

19 = 10 + 9, dix–neuf

All the numbers between 21 and 69 follow a similar pattern. In French, the numbers 21, 31, 41, 51, and 61 are joined with the conjunction "*and*" or "*et*", as in *vingt–et–un*. As in English, the rest of the numbers are separated by hyphens.

21 – vingt–et–un /vɛ̃t e ɛ̃/

22 – vingt–deux /vɛ̃ dø/

23 – vingt–trois /vɛ̃ trwa/

24 – vingt–quatre /vɛ̃ katr/

25 – vingt–cinq /vɛ̃ sɛ̃k/

26 – vingt–six /vɛ̃ sis/

27 – vingt–sept /vɛ̃ sɛt/

28 – vingt–huit /vɛ̃ ɥi(t)/

29 – vingt–neuf /v□□ nœf/

There's no language that uses the same number system as French. Until 60, everything looks pretty standard, but then math takes over.

70 represents the addition of 60 and 10. And the moment you think you've got this pattern, it suddenly changes with the next number. 80 instead of addition relies on multiplication (4x20), while 90 represents the higher math problem 4x20+10.

30 – trente /tʁɑ̃t/

40 – quarante /kaʁɑ̃t/

50 – cinquante /sɛ̃kɑ̃t/

60 – soixante /swasɑ̃t/

70 – soixante–dix /swasɑ̃tdis/ actually 60 + 10

80 – quatre–vingt /katʁəvɛ̃/

90 – quatre–vingt–dix /katʁəvɛ̃dis/

100 – cent /sɛnt/

1000 – mille /mil/

From 100 – 199

Use *cent* followed by the remaining number.

105 = cent–cinq /sɛnt sɛ̃k/

144 = cent–quarante–quatre /sɛnt kaʀɑ̃t katr/

181 = cent–quatre–vingt–un /sɛnt katr/

From 200 – 999

This part is relatively simple as it follows the same pattern.

200 – deux–cents /dø sɛnt/

300 – trois–cents /trwa sɛnt/

400 – quatre–cents /katr sɛnt/

500 – cinq–cents etc. /sɛ̃k sɛnt/

Ordinal Numbers

A noun's ordinal number indicates its position in a sequence (e.g. the first car on your left, the second house on the right). Most ordinal numbers go with both masculine and feminine words.

The important exception is "first" where we use two forms, "*première*" for feminine nouns and "*premier*" for masculine nouns.

la cinquième maison /la sɛ̃kjɛm mezɔ̃/– the fifth house

la première chanteuse /la p□□mjer □□□tœz/ – the first singer

first – **premier/première** /pʀəmje – pʀəmjer/

second – **deuxième** /døzjɛm/

third – **troisième** /tʀwazjɛm/

48

fourth – **quatrième** /katʀijɛm/

fifth – **cinquième** /sɛ̃kjɛm/

sixth – **sixième** /sizjɛm/

seventh – **septième** /sɛtjɛm/

eighth – **huitième** /ɥitjɛm/

ninth – **neuvième** /nœvj□m/

tenth – **dixième** /dizjɛm/

eleventh – **onzième** /ɔ̃zjɛm/

twelfth – **douzième** /duzjɛm/

thirteenth – **treizième** /tʀɛzjɛm/

fourteenth – **quatorzième** /katɔʀzjɛm/

fifteenth – **quinzième** /kɛ̃zjɛm/

sixteenth – **seizième** /sɛzjɛm/

seventeenth – **dix–septième** /di(s)sɛtjɛm/

eighteenth – **dix–huitième** /dizɥitjɛm/

nineteenth – **dix–neuvième** /diznœvj□m/

twentieth – **vingtième** /vɛ̃tjɛm/

Chapter 4: Greetings and Civilities

Il nous faut accepter de dire au revoir à la vie que nous avions imaginée, pour laisser place à celle qui nous attend.

E.M.Foster

Every encounter with a French person has its own social etiquette. Depending on the context, formal or informal setting, you may opt for a firm handshake or a kiss if you are meeting French people.

A typical French greeting is a kiss (*la bise*). *La bise* can include one, two, or even three small kisses on the cheek, depending on the region. When in doubt, let the other person initiate kisses, and remember that kisses generally begin on the right side.

However, in a formal or business environment, you would not do this, and instead you would use a firm handshake. Men are also more likely to greet with a handshake than a *bise*. As a woman, you are permitted to kiss both male and female friends, acquaintances, and family members, even with people you are still not familiar with. As a guy, you can have a *bise* with female friends, associates, and family members. For two adult males, however, it is not usual to faire *la bise*, but it does happen from time to time.

Hugging French is a tricky area. In fact, hugging in France is not common between friends or even family members. It's interesting that French don't even have a word for hug, at least not in the same sense. The closest translation would be to simply "*take someone in your arms*" or "*prendre dans les bras*" or "*faire un câlin*" but both refer to a romantic gesture. It's more like a tender hug between a couple. Contrary to American greetings, hugging is reserved for children or significant others only.

Greetings

The most common French greeting is *"bonjour"* (hello). You can use *bonjour* to say "good morning" or "hello", when you meet someone for the first time of the day.

Bonjour /bɔ̃ʒuʀ/– Hello! (also good morning)

Bonsoir /bɔ̃swaʀ/ – Good evening!

Salut /saly/ – Hi! or Goodbye! (informal) also appropriate when you see someone again later in the day.

Coucou /kuku/ – Hey there! (close friends use this casual salutation)

Âllo /alo/ – Hello (when answering the phone)

Au revoir ! /ʀəvwaʀ/ – Goodbye!

Bonne journée ! /bɔ̃ ʒuʀne/ – Good day!

Bon après–midi ! /bɔ̃ apʀɛmidi/ – Good afternoon! (After 12:00 pm)

Bonne soirée ! /bɔ̃ swaʀe/ – Good evening!

Bonne nuit ! /bɔ̃ nɥi/ – Good night !

À plus tard ! /a ply taʀ/ – See you later!

À toute à l'heure ! /atu ta lœ□/ – See you soon!

À bientôt ! /a bjɛ̃to/ – See you soon!

À demain ! /a də.mɛ̃/ – See you tomorrow!

How are you?

After greeting someone, you should always ask *"How are you?"* as it is considered rude to skip this question. There are a lot of phrases for checking in with someone, and you'll notice that contrary to English, all questions contain the verb *"aller"* (to go) instead of *"être"* (to be).

When asked how you are, the most common responses are *"Ça va bien"* ("It's going well") or *"Tout va bien"* ("Everything's going well"). Similarly to English, it is uncommon to respond, "ça va mal" even if you aren't at your best.

You can address people formally (using *Vous*) or informally (using *Tu*).

Comment ça va ? /kɔmã sa va/ – How are you? (neutral)

Ça va ? /sa va/ – How are you doing? (condensed version of the question "Comment ça va ?")

Comment allez-vous ? /kɔmã ale vu/ – How are you? (formal)

Tu vas bien ? /ty va bjẽ/ – Are you doing well? (polite way to ask someone when you're expecting a positive reply).

Quoi de neuf ? /kwa də nœf/ – What's up? (very casual option to say hello in French, used only with close friends).

Et toi ? /etwa/ – And you ? (informal)

Et vous? /evu/ – And you ? (formal)

Here are the ways you can answer the above mentioned questions.

> **Bien, merci !** /bjẽ mɛʀsi/ – Good, thanks!
>
> **Très bien, merci.** /tʀɛ bjẽ mɛʀsi / – Very well, thanks.
>
> **Ça va.** /sa va/ – I'm good.
>
> **Ça roule.** /sa ʀule/ – It's going well.
>
> **Comme–ci, comme–ça.** /kɔm si kɔm sa/ – So, so.
>
> **Pas mal.** /pa mal/ – Not bad.
>
> **Pas pire que d'habitude.** /pas piʀ ke dabityd/ – No worse than usual.

Comme d'habitude. /kɔm dabityd/ – Same as always.

Assez bien. /ase bjɛ̃/ – Quite well.

Ça va bien. /sa va bjɛ̃/ – It's going well.

Tout va bien. /tu va bjɛ̃/ – Everything's going well.

Leaving

Je suis désolé(e), mais je dois y aller. /ʒə sɥi dezɔle, mɛ ʒə dwa i ale/ – I'm sorry, but I have to go.

Désolé(e), mais je dois filer ! /dezɔle mɛ ʒə dwa file/ – Sorry, but I gotta run! (informal)

Je n'ai pas le temps. /ʒə nɛ pa lə tã/ – I don't have time.

Excuse moi, je suis pressé(e). /ɛkskyze mwa ʒə sɥi prese/ – Excuse me, I am in a rush.

On se voit demain à… /ɔ̃ sə vwa d(ə)mɛ̃ a/ – See you tomorrow at…

Je t'appelle. /ʒə tap(ə)le/ – I'll call you.

Dites-leur bonjour de ma part. /dit lœ□ b□□□u□ d ma par/ – Say hello to them for me.

Basic Courtesy

People in France are actually some of the most polite and courteous people in the world. In France, being polite is incredibly important, and everyone adheres to it. The simplest of *bonjour*, followed by *Madame/Monsieur* could open doors for you.

Whenever you enter a shop, say *bonjour* to the shopkeeper; when you board a bus, say *bonjour* to the driver; when you arrive at work, say *bonjour* to your colleagues. You can also use basic words such as "*merci*" and "*s'il vous plaît*" liberally.

Thanking

Merci. /mɛʀsi/ – Thank you.

Non merci. /nɔ̃ mɛʀsi/ – No, thank you.

Merci beaucoup. /mɛʀsi boku/ – Thank you very much.

Merci bien. /mɛʀsi bjɛ̃/ – Thank you very much.

Mille fois merci. /mil fwa mɛʀsi/ – Thank you so much. (Literally means "a thousand times thank you")

Je l'apprecie. /ʒə lapresi/ – I appreciate it.

Merci de votre aide. /mɛʀsi də votʀ ɛd/ – Thank you for your help.

De rien. /də ʀjɛ̃/ – You are welcome.

Pas de quoi. /pa də kwa / – Don't mention it.

Je vous en prie. /ʒə vuz ã pri/ – It was my pleasure. (formal)

Je t'en prie. /ʒə tã pri/ – My pleasure. (informal)

S'il vous plaît. /sil vu plɛ/ – Please. (formal)

S'il te plaît. /sil tə plɛ/ – Please. (informal)

Vous êtes très gentil(le). /vuzet tʀɛ ʒãti/ – *You are very kind.*

Apologies, Misunderstandings and Regrets

Excusez–moi. /ɛkskyze mwa/ – Excuse me.

Excusez–moi de vous déranger. /ɛkskyze mwa də vu deʀãʒe/ – I am sorry to disturb you.

Pardon. /paʀdɔ̃/ – I beg your pardon. (on the street)

Pardonnez–moi. /paʀdɔne mwa/ – Forgive me.

Je suis desolé(é). /ʒə sчi dezɔle/ – I am sorry. (used to say sorry for something you have done)

Excusez–moi un instant. /□kskyze mwa œ□ □□st□□/ – Excuse me for a moment.

Excusez–mon retard. /ɛkskyze mɔ̃ ʀ(ə)taʀ/ – Forgive me for being late.

Excusez–moi, j'ai besoin de... /ɛkskyze mwa ʒɛ bəzwɛ̃ d/ – Excuse me, I need...

Excusez–moi, je n'ai pas bien compris. /ɛkskyze mwa ʒ nɛ pa bjɛ̃ kɔ̃pʀi/ – Excuse me, I didn't quite understand.

Ne vous inquiétez pas. /n vuz ɛ̃kjete pa/ – Do not worry.

Je n'ai pas voulu vous offenser. /ʒə nɛ pa volu vuz ɔfãse/ – I didn't mean to offend you.

Ça doit être une erreur. /sa dwa □t□ yn e□œ□/ – It has to be a mistake.

J'ai fait une erreur. Je me suis trompé(e). /□□f□ yn e□œ□/ /ʒɛ mə sɥi tʀɔ̃pe/ – I made a mistake.

Malheureusement oui/non. /maløʀøzmã wi/no/ – Unfortunately yes/no.

Requests, Orders and Suggestions

Pouvez-vous m'aider ? /puve vu mede/ – Can you help me?

Pourrais-je (avoir)... ? – /puʀe ʒɛ avwaʀ/ – Can l have... ?

Pourriez–vous me dire ? /puʀje vu mə diʀ/ – Could you tell me?

J'aimerais vous demander ... /ʒɛmʀɛ vu demande/ – I would like to ask you...

J'aimerais / Je voudrais.. /ʒɛmʀɛ / ʒɛ vudʀɛ/ – I would like....

Pourriez vous me donner un conseil ? – /puʀje vu m□ done œ□ k□□s□j/ – Could you give me an advice?

Serait-il possible de... ? /sɛʀɛt il pɔsibl də/ – Would it be possible to... ?

Je voudrais parler à/avec... /ʒɛ vudʀɛ paʀle a/avɛk/ – I would like to talk with...

Je voudrais prendre un rendez–vous. /□□ vudʀ□ p□□□□d□ œ□ □□□devu/ – I would like to take an appointment.

Pouvez-vous attendre un moment ? /puve vu at□□d□ œ□ m□m□□/ – Could you wait for a moment?

Je pourrais l'emprunter ? /ʒɛ puʀe l□□p□œ□te/ – Could I borrow it?

Je peux me joindre à vous ? /ʒɛ p vu ʒwɛ̃dʀ/ – Could I join you?

Vous viendrez me chercher ? /vu vjɛ̃dʀe m ʃɛʀʃe/ – Will you pick me up?

Pouvez-vous me passer ? /puve vu m pase/ – Could you pass me?

Je voudrais savoir si... /ʒə vudʀɛ savwaʀ si/ – I would like to know if...

Vous pouvez vous renseigner là-dessus ? /vu puve vu ʀɑ̃seɲe la dəsy/ – Can you find out about it?

Excusez–moi, j'ai besoin de... /ɛkskuze mwa ʒɛ bəzwɛ̃ də/ – Excuse me, I need to...

Je peux vous aider ? /□□ pœ vuz□de/ – Can I help you ?

Je cherche... /ʒə ʃɛʀʃ/ – I am looking for...

Pouvez-vous m'y conduire ? /puve vu mi kɔ̃dɥiʀ/ – Can you drive me there?

Voulez–vous ? /vule vu/ – Do you want to?

Voulez–vous vous joindre à nous ? /vule vu nu ʒwɛ̃dʀ/ – Do you want to join us?

Ça vous gêne si... ? /sa vu ʒen si/ – Does it bother you if... ?

Si ça ne vous gêne pas. /si sa n vu ʒen pa/ – If you don't mind.

Vous êtes d'accord ? /vuzɛt dakɔʀ/ – Do you agree?

Vous en êtes sûr(e) ? /vuz ã ɛt syr/ – Are you sure?

Pourquoi pas ? /puʀkwa pa/ – Why not?

Attendez un moment, s'il vous plaît. /atɑ̃de œ̃ mɔmɑ̃ sil vu plɛ/ – Wait a moment, please.

Vous pouvez entrer. /vu puve ɑ̃tʀe/ – You can come in.

Entrez, s'il vous plaît. /ɑ̃tʀe sil vu plɛ/ – Please come in.

Débarrassez–vous. /debaʀase vu/ – Take your coat/jacket off.

Asseyez-vous ! /aseje vu/ – Sit down!

Mettez–vous à l'aise ! /mete vu alɛz/ – Make yourself comfortable.

Qu'est–ce que je vous sers ? /kɛsk ʒ vu ser/ – What can I get you?

Servez–vous. /sɛrve vu/ – Help yourself.

Ressers–toi. /ʀ(ə)ser twa/ – Help yourself to more food.

Agreement and Disagreement

Agreement

Oui. /wi/ – Yes.

Bien sûr. Naturellement. /bjɛ̃ syr natyʀɛlmɑ̃/ – Of course. Naturally.

Bien entendu. Evidemment. /bjɛ̃ ɑ̃tɑ̃dy evidamɑ̃/ – Of course. Obviously.

Sans doute. Bien sûr. /sɑ̃ dut bjɛ̃ syr/ – No doubt. Of course.

Avec plaisir. /avɛk plezir/ – With pleasure.

D'accord. /dakɔʀ/ – All right.

Pourquoi pas ? /puʀkwa pa/ – Why not?

Je crois que oui. /ʒə kʀwa k wi/ – I think so.

Vous avez raison. /vuzave ʀezɔ̃/ – You are right.

C'est vrai. /sɛ vʀɛ/ – It's true.

Bonne idée. /bon ide/ – Good idea.

Pas de problème. /pas də pʀɔblɛm/ – No problem.

Sans problème. /sã pʀɔblɛm/ – No problem.

Peut–être. /pøtɛtʀ/ – Maybe.

Ça a l'air bien. /sa a lɛʀ bjɛ̃/ – It sounds good.

Disagreement

Non. /nɔ̃/ – No.

Non, merci. /nɔ̃ mɛʀsi/ – No, thank you.

Certainement pas. /sɛʀtɛnmã pa/ – Certainly not.

Pas moi. /pa mwa/ – Not me.

Pas pour moi. /pa puʀ mwa/ – Not for me.

Je ne suis pas d'accord avec vous. /ʒə nə sɥi pa dakɔʀ avɛk vu/ – I don't agree with you.

Ce n'est pas vrai. /sə nɛ pa vʀɛ/ – That's not true.

Pas du tout. /pa dy tu/ – Not at all.

En aucun cas. /□□ okœ□ ka/ – Under no circumstances.

Jamais. /ʒamɛ/ – Never.

Absolument pas. /apsɔlymã pa/ – Absolutely not.

Ça doit être une erreur. /sa dwat □t□ yn e□œ□/ – It must be a mistake.

Malheureusement, je ne peux pas. /maløʀøzmɑ̃ ʒə nə pø pa/ – Unfortunately, I can't.

Je dois refuser. /ʒə dwa ʀefyze/ – I have to refuse.

Je ne peux pas accepter. /ʒə nə pø pa aksɛpte/ – I can not accept.

Peut-être la prochaine fois. /pøtɛtʀ la pʀɔʃɛ̃ fwa/– Maybe next time.

Wishes and Holiday Greetings

Santé ! /sɑ̃te/ – Cheers!

Félicitations ! /felisitasjɔ̃/ – Congratulations!

Bonne chance ! /bɔ̃ ʃɑ̃s/ – Good luck!

Bon voyage ! /bɔn vwajaʒ/ – Have a nice trip!

Bon anniversaire !/bɔn anivɛʀsɛʀ/ – Happy birthday!

Amusez-vous bien ! /amuze vu bjɛ̃/ – Have a good time!

Rentrez bien ! /ʀɑ̃tʀe bjɛ̃/ – Safe travel!

Joyeuses fêtes ! /ʒwa.jøz fɛt/ – Happy holidays!

Bonnes Fêtes ! /bɔn fɛt/ – Happy Holidays!

Meilleurs Vœux ! /m□jœ□ vø/ – Best Wishes!

Je vous souhaite de joyeuses fêtes ! /ʒə vu swet də ʒwajøz fɛt/ – I wish you happy holidays!

Bonne Année ! /bɔn ane/ – Happy New Year!

Meilleurs vœux pour la nouvelle année ! /m□jœ□ vø pu□ la nuvel ane/ – Best wishes for the New Year!

Joyeux Noël ! /ʒwajø nɔɛl/ – Merry Christmas!

Joyeux Noël à toi et à tes proches ! /ʒwajø nɔɛl a twa e te pʀɔʃ/ – Merry Christmas to you and your loved ones!

Joyeuses Pâques ! */ʒwajøz pak/* – Happy Easter!

Chapter 5: Meeting People

Tomber amoureux, c'est facile. Faire l'amour encore plus. Mais rencontrer quelqu'un qui t'allume l'âme, ça, c'est exceptionnel.

Adelaire Landay

You'll easily meet French people in a group of friends, by simply asking their name or introducing yourself first. While waiting for a bus or queuing, it may be possible to meet someone randomly, but French people prefer silence and don't like to disturb others, so starting a deep conversation in such places may be considered rude, especially if that person isn't willing to proceed with the communication. Unlike Americans, who immediately present their name, where they are from, their job, the French consider those things quite personal. Be careful not to reveal too much about yourself too soon because it may scare some of them. In France, conversations grow as you become more familiar with each other. If you're new to France and want to meet French people, language exchange events are a good place to start as they usually lead to exchanging numbers and hanging out afterward.

What is Your Name?

Comment vous appelez vous ? /kɒmɛnt vuzap(ə)levu/ – What is your name? (formal)

Comment t'appelles tu ? /kɒmɛnt tap(ə)le ty/ – What's your name? (informal)

Quel est votre prénom ? /kɛl e tɔ̃ pʀenɔ̃/ – What's your name? (formal)

Quel est votre nom ? /kɛl e vɔtʀ nɔ̃/ – What's your last name? (formal)

Quel est ton prénom ? /kɛl e tɔ̃ pʀenɔ̃/ – What's your name? (informal)

Quel est ton nom ? /kɛl e tɔ̃ nɔ̃/ – What's your last name? (informal)

Introducing Yourself

Je m'appelle, _ . /ʒə mapɛl/ – My name is _ .

Je suis _ . /ʒə sɥi/ – I am _ .

Mon nom est _ . /mɔ̃ nɔ̃ ɛ / – My name is _

Mon prénom est _ . /mɔ̃ pʀenɔ̃ ɛ/ – My first name is _

Moi, c'est _ . /mwa sɛ/ – By the way, I'm _ . (informal) (used when the other person's name is said first).

Je m'appelle _ , mais je me fais appeler _ . /ʒə mapɛl _ mɛ ʒə mə fɛ apəle _/ – My name is (name), but I prefer to be called (nickname).

Je me présente. Je m'appelle/Je suis _ . /ʒə m pʀezɑ̃te. ʒə mapɛl _ . or ʒə sɥi _ / – Allow me to introduce myself. My name is/I'm _ . (very formal)

Introducing Others

Comment s'appelle _ ? /kɒmɛnt sapəle/ – What's . . . name?

Example:

Comment s'appelle ta fille ? /kɒmɛnt sapəle ta fij/ – What's your daughter's name?

→ **Formal**

   Je vous présente (name). /ʒə vu pʀezɑ̃te/ – Allow me to introduce (name).

Je te présente (name). /ʒə tə pʀezɑ̃te/ – Allow me to introduce (name).

Example:

Je vous présente Marie. Marie est actrice. /ʒə vu pʀezɑ̃te Mari. Mari ɛ aktʀis/ – Allow me to introduce Marie. Marie is an actress. (This is often followed by a brief explanation of who the person is).

→ **Informal**

The word "*voici*" can be used to introduce a person that's located near us, or to introduce a new person.

Voici (name). /vwasi _ /– This is (name).

Example:

Voici Marie. /vwasi Mari/– This is Marie.

When we introduce someone who is not physically near us, we have two common options.

Ça, c'est (name). /sa sɛ _/ – That person there is (name). Note that this phrase can be followed with additional information.

Example:

Ça, c'est Marie. Elle est française. – That person there is Marie. She's French.

Voilà _. /vwala/ – That's (name).

Example:

Voilà Jean. – That's Jean.

Note * we use **Voilà/Voici** to introduce things too.

Pleasure to Meet You

→ Informally you can just say:

Enchanté(e) /ãʃãte/ – Pleasure.

→ Formally:

C'est un plaisir de vous rencontrer. /sɛt an pleziʀ də vu ʀãkɔ̃tʀe/ – It's a pleasure to meet you. (formal version)

Enchanté(e) de faire votre connaissance. /ãʃãte də fɛʀ vɔtʀ kɔnɛsãs/ – Pleased to meet you.

C'est un plaisir de faire votre connaissance. /sɛt an pleziʀ də fɛʀ vɔtʀ kɔnɛsãs/ – It is a pleasure to meet you.

Personal Data – Filling in Forms

Many places require you to fill out forms and provide personal information, such as applying for a job, opening a bank account, getting insurance, and going to the hospital. Below is the most common data you'll need to enter.

les données personnelles /le done pɛʀsɔnɛl/ – personal data

le prénom et nom /pʀenõ / nõ/ – name and last name

la date de naissance /la dat d nɛsãs/ – the birth date

le lieu de naissance /lə ljø d nɛsãs/ – the birth place

l'état de santé /leta d sante/ – health status

la situation familiale /la sitɥasjõ d famij/ – family status

> **célibataire** /selibatɛʀ/ – single

> **marié(e)** /maʀje/ – married

> **divorcé(e)** /divɔʀse/ – divorced

l'adresse /ladʀɛs/ – adresse

> **permanente** /pɛʀmanãt/ – permanent

> **provisoire/actuelle** /pʀɔvizwar /aktɥɛl/ – current

le numéro de téléphone /lə numero d telefɔn/ – telephone number

l'adresse électronique /ladʀɛs elɛktʀɔnik/ – the email address

la formation /la fɔʀmasjɔ̃/ – education

le parcours professionnel /lə parkur pʀɔfesjɔnɛl/ – professional background

l'expérience professionnelle /lɛkspeʀjãs pʀɔfesjɔnɛl/ – professional experience

le permis de conduire /lə pɛʀmi də kɔ̃dɥiʀ/ – the driving license

la date de disponibilité /la dat də dispɔnibilite/ – availability date

Do You Understand?

The French word for understand is *"comprendre"*. To say you *don't understand*, you have to use the negative *ne + pas* formation.

Est-ce que vous comprenez ? /ɛskə vu kɔ̃pʀãne/ – Do you understand? (formal)

Est–ce que tu comprends ? /ɛskə ty kɔ̃pʀãn/ – Do you understand? (informal)

    Oui, je comprend. /wi ʒə kɔ̃pʀãn/ – Yes, I understand.

    Excusez–moi, je ne comprends pas. /ɛkskyze mwa ʒə nə kɔ̃pʀãn pa/ – *Sorry, I don't understand.*

Pouvez-vous répéter, s'il vous plaît ? /puvevu repete sil vu plɛ/ – Can you repeat, please? (formal)

Peux-tu répéter, s'il te plaît? /pœ ty repete sil tə plɛ/ – Can you repeat, please? (informal)

Comment dit–on ... en français ? /kɔmã dit ɔ̃n ... ã fʀãsɛ/– How do you say ... in French?

You could also change the word order slightly and say:

Ça se dit comment en français ? /sa sə di kɔmã ã fʁãsɛ/ – How do you say that in French?

Pouvez-vous parler plus lentement, s'il vous plaît ? /puvevu parle ply lãtmã sil vu plɛ/ – Can you speak more slowly, please?

You could replace "parler" with "répéter"– to repeat.

Pouvez-vous répéter plus lentement, s'il vous plaît ? /puvevu repete ply lãtmã sil vu plɛ/ – *Can you say that again more slowly, please?*

You can also ask someone to repeat themselves in less formal ways:

Qu'est–ce que t'as dit ? /kɛskə ta di/ – What did you say?

Comment ? /kɔmã/ – What was that?

Quoi ? /kwa/ – What?

How Old Are You?

In French, expressing your age differs in one word from English. French uses the verb "to have" instead of the verb "to be".

Quel âge as–tu ? /kɛl aʒ a ty/ – How old are you? (informal)

Quel âge avez-vous ? /kɛl aʒ ave vu/ – How old are you? (formal)

> **J'ai** (number of years) **ans.** /ʒe (...) ã/ – I am (number of years). Literally translated, it means "I have + age").
>
> Example:

J'ai vingt-deux ans. /ʒe vɛ̃døzã/ – I am 22 years old.

Where Do You Live?

Où habites–tu ? */u abit ty/* – Where do you live? (informal)

Où habitez-vous ? */u abite vu/* – Where do you live? (formal)

J'habite à Paris. */ʒəabite a Pari/* – I live in Paris.

J'habite en France. */ʒəabite ã fʀãs/* – l live in France.

D'où venez-vous ? */du vəne vu/* – Where do you come from? (formal)

D'où viens–tu ? */du vjẽ ty/* – Where do you come from? (informal)

Je viens de Paris. */ʒə vjẽ də Pari/* – I come from Paris.

Je viens de France. */ʒə vjẽ də fʀãs/* – I come from France.

Note that we use different prepositions according to genre and number of a country.

- For cities/towns/villages, use *à*:

J'habite à Rome. – I live in Rome.

- For feminine countries (countries ending with the letter –e), use *en*:

J'étudie en France. – I study in France.

- For masculine countries (i.e. not ending with –e or –s), use *au*:

Je travaille au Brésil. – I work in Brazil.

- For plural countries (i.e. ending with –s), use *aux* (the –x is silent):

Je suis né(e) aux Pays-Bas. – I was born in the Netherlands.

Continents

l'**Afrique** /lafʀik/ – Africa

l'**Europe** /løʀɔp/ – Europe

l'**Asie** /lazi/ – Asia

l'**Océanie** /lɔseani/ – Oceania

l'**Amérique** /lameʀik/ – America

l'**Australie** /ostʀali/ – Australia

l'**Antarctique** /lɑ☐taʀktik/ – Antarctica

Countries, Languages and Nationalities

	Country	Language	Nationality
Algeria	l'**Algérie** (f.) /alʒeʀi/	l'arabe /laʀab/	*Algérien(ne)* /alʒeʀjɛ☐/
Austria	l'**Autriche** /otʀiʃ/	l'allemand /lalma☐/	Autrichien(ne) /otʀiʃjɛ☐/
Germany	l'**Allemagne** (f.) /almaɲ/	l'allemand	Allemande /lalma☐/
Belgium	la **Belgique** /bɛlʒik/	le belge /bɛlʒ/	Belge /bɛlʒ/
Brazil	le **Brésil** /bʀezil/	*le portugais* /pɔʀtygɛ/	Brésilienne(ne) /bʀeziljɛ☐/

68

Canada	**le Canada** /kanada/	le français /fʀa□sɛ/	*Canadien(ne)* /kanadjɛ□/
China	**la Chine** /la ʃin/	le chinois /ʃinwa/	Chinois(e) /ʃinwa/
Denmark	**le Danemark** /danmaʀk/	le danois /danwa/	Danois(e) /danwa/
United States	**les États–Unis** (m.) /etazyni/	l'anglais / a□glɛ/	Américain(e) /amerikɛ□/
Egypt	**l'Égypte** (f.) /eʒipt/	l'arabe /laʀab/	*Égyptien(ne)* /eʒipsjɛ□/
Spain	**l'Espagne** /ɛspaɲ/	l'espagnol /ɛspaɲɔl/	Espagnol(e) /ɛspaɲɔl/
England	**l'Angleterre** (f.) /a□glətɛʀ/	l'anglais	Anglais(e)
France	**la France** /fʀa□s/	le français /fʀa□sɛ/	Français(e) /fʀa□sɛ/
Greece	**la Grèce** /ˈgriːs/	le grec /gʀɛk/	Grec(que) /gʀɛk/

Hungary	**La Hongrie** /ɔ□gʀi/	le hongrois /ɔ□gʀwa/	hongrois(e) /ɔ□gʀwa/
India	**l'Inde** (f.) /ɛ□d/	*l'hindi* /lɪndi/	Indien(ne) /ɛ□djɛ□/
Israel	**l'Israël** (m.) /isʀaɛl/	l'hébreu /lebʀø/	Israélien(ne) /Isʀaeljɛ□/
Italy	**l'Italie** (f.) /itali/	l'italien /Italjɛ□/	Italien(ne) /Italjɛ□/
Ireland	**l'Irlande** (f.) /iʀla□d/	l'irlandais /Iʀla□dɛ/	Irlandais(e) /Iʀla□dɛ/
Iran	**l'Iran** (m.) /iʀa□/	le perse /lə pɛrsə/	Iranien(ne) /iʀanjɛ□/
Japan	**le Japon** /ʒapɔ□/	e japonais /ʒapɔnɛ/	Japonais(e) /ʒapɔnɛ/
Mexico	**le Mexique** /mɛksik/	l'espagnol /ɛspaɲɔl/	Mexicain(e) /mɛksikɛ□/
Netherlands	**les Pays–Bas** /peiba/	le néerlandais /neɛʀla□dɛ/	*Néerlandais(e)* /neɛʀla□dɛ/

New Zealand	**la Nouvelle–Zélande** /nuvɛlzela□d/	l'anglais	Néo–zélandais(e) /neo–zela□de/
Sweden	**la Suède** /sɥɛd/	le suédois /sɥedwa/	Suédois(e) /sɥedwa/
Portugal	**le Portugal** /pɔʀtygal/	le portugais /pɔʀtygɛ/	Portugais(e) /pɔʀtygɛ/
United Kingdom	**le Royaume–Uni** /ʀwajomyni/	l'anglais	anglais(e)
Russia	**la Russie** /ʀysi/	le russe /ʀys/	Russe /ʀys/
Turkey	**la Turquie** /tyʀki/	le turc /tyʀk/	Turque /tyʀk/
Tunisia	**la Tunisie** /tynizi/	L'arabe /aʀab/	Tunisien(ne) /tynizjɛ□/
United Arab Emirates	**les Émirats arabes unis** /lezemiʀaaʀab yni/	l'arabe	Arabe

Nationalities

Quelle est ta nationalité ? /kɛl ɛ ta nasjɔnalite/ – What's your nationality?

> **Je suis français.** /ʒə sɥi fʀɑ̃sɛ/ – I am French. (if you are a man)

> **Je suis française.** /ʒə sɥi fʀɑ̃sez/ – I am French. (if you are a woman)

> **Je ne suis pas française.** /ʒə nə sɥi pa fʀɑ̃sɛ/ – I am not French.

As you can see, the pronunciation differs slightly if you are a woman or a man. That's because the additional –e you add to all feminine forms turns the silent consonant into a pronounced one. It happens with the letters "t" and "n".

Languages

When you are making French friends, they may also be curious about your abilities to learn new languages and how many languages you know. So it can be part of the introduction.

Quelles langues parles–tu ? /kɛl lɑ̃g parl ty/ – What languages do you speak?

Quelles langues parlez–vous ? /kɛl lɑ̃g parle vu/ – What languages do you speak?

> **Je parle français et anglais.** /ʒə parl fʀɑ̃sɛ e ɑ̃glɛ/ – I speak French and English.

> **J'étudie l'allemand.** /ʒə etydje almɑ̃ / – I am studying German.

> **J'apprends le Français depuis 3 mois.** /ʒə apʀɑ̃d lə fʀɑ̃sɛ dəpɥi tʀwa mwa/– I have been learning French for 3 months.

Parlez–vous français ? /paʀle vu fʀɑ̃sɛ/ – Do you speak French?

> **Oui, je parle français.** /wi ʒə parl fʀɑ̃sɛ/ – Yes, I speak French.

> **Non, je ne parle pas français.** /no ʒə nə parl pa fʀɑ̃sɛ/ – No, I don't speak French.

Est-ce qu'il y a quelqu'un qui parle anglais ? /□skilja k□lkœ□ ki parl ɑ̃glɛ/ – Is there anyone who speaks English?

Oui, moi je parle français. /wi mwa ʒə parl fʀɑ̃sɛ/ – Yes, I speak French.

Personne ne parle français ici. /pɛʀsɔn nə parl fʀɑ̃sɛ isi/ – No one speaks French here.

Chapter 6: Time

Au lieu de regarder le temps qui passe, il vaut mieux l'utiliser.

Nouredine Meftah

There is also a cultural aspect to arriving on time or being late. For Americans, it is proper etiquette to arrive on time for a dinner. While that is the custom in America, in France, arriving on time to a dinner party is considered rude. It is likely that the host will still be preparing for the dinner party if you arrive early or on time. Arriving 15 minutes late to a party is proper etiquette.

You may be surprised to learn that shops and markets do not operate on Sundays, or if they do, they have shortened hours. Also, there are few shops with 24–hour shifts. Make sure you plan your grocery shopping accordingly.

Days, Weeks

aujourd'hui /oʒuʀdɥi/ – today

hier /jɛʀ/– yesterday

demain /dəmɛ̃/– tomorrow

le lendemain /lɑ̃dmɛ̃/– the day after, the next day

avant–hier /avɑ̃tjɛʀ/– the day before yesterday

après–demain /apʀɛdəmɛ̃/ – the day after tomorrow

maintenant /mɛ̃tənɑ̃/– now

dans la journée /dɑ̃ la ʒuʀne/ – during the day

une fois par jour /yn fwa par ʒuʀ/ – once a day

dans trois jours /dɑ̃ tʀwa ʒuʀ/ – in three days

tous les jours /tu le ʒuʀ/ – everyday

tous les matins /tu le matɛ̃/ – every morning

à midi /a midi/ – at noon

ce soir /sə swaʀ/ – tonight

hier soir /jɛʀ swaʀ/ – yesterday evening

à/après minuit /a/apʀɛ minɥi/ – at/after midnight

la semaine passée/dernière /la s(ə)mɛn pase/dɛʀnje/ – last week

la semaine prochaine /la s(ə)mɛn pʀɔʃɛ̃/ – next week

une fois /yn fwa/ – once

une fois par semaine /yn fwa paʀ səmɛn/ – once a week

deux fois par semaine /dø fwa paʀ səmɛn/ – twice a week

un jour férié /ʒuʀ feʀje/ – a holiday

une journée de travail /ʒuʀne də tʀavaj/ – a working day

le crépuscule /lə kʀepyskyl/ – dusk

l'aube /lob/ – dawn

Parts of the Day

If you get confused when you see, *"journée"* and *"jour"*, *"soirée"* and *"soir"*, *"matinée"* and *"matin"*, *"année"* and *"an"*, know that the second word refers to what we mean by regular day/morning in English, while the first word (journée, soirée, matinée and année) explains the passing of time more subjectively.

un jour /ʒuʀ/ – a day

une journée /ʒuʀne/ – the day, duration of time

matin /matɛ̃/ – morning

la matinée /matine/ – morning (focusing on the duration of time)

le matin /lə matɛ̃/ – in the morning

le midi /midi/ – noon

l'après–midi /apʀɛmidi/ – afternoon

soir /swaʀ/ – evening

la soirée /swaʀe/ – evening (duration of time)

le soir /swaʀ/ – in the evening

la nuit /nɥi/ – night

minuit /minɥi/ – midnight

Days of the Week

Semaine /səmɛn/ – week

Lundi /lœ☐di/ – Monday

Mardi /maʀdi/ – Tuesday

Mercredi /mɛʀkʀədi/– Wednesday

Jeudi /ʒødi/ – Thursday

Vendredi /vãdʀədi/ – Friday

Samedi /samdi/ – Saturday

Dimanche /dimãʃ/ – Sunday

Date

When it comes to telling the date, there are several ways to do it.

- **C'est + le + number + month.**

C'est le quatorze juillet. /sɛ lə katɔʀz ʒɥijɛ/ – It's July 14th.

It applies to all days of the month except the first. To say the first of the month, say "*premier*".

C'est le premier janvier. /sɛ lə pʀəmje ʒa☐vje/ – It's January 1st.

- **Nous sommes + le + number + month.** – We are on + date.

Nous sommes le 2 avril. /nu som lə second avril/– We are April 2nd.

- **On est + le + number + month.** – We are on + date. (impersonal)

- On est le 10 november. /ɔ̃ e lə dis nɔvãbʀ/ – It is November 10th.

Asking About Date

Quelle date sommes–nous aujourd'hui ? /kɛl dat som nu oʒuʀdɥi/ – What's the date today?

On est le sept juin. – It is June 7th.

Quel jour sommes–nous ?

> **Aujourd'hui c'est lundi.** /o☐u☐d☐i s☐ lœ☐di/ – Today, it's Monday.

> **Aujourd'hui on est lundi.** /o☐u☐d☐i ☐☐ ☐ lœ☐di/ – Today is Monday.

En quel mois sommes–nous ?

> **Nous sommes en janvier.** /nu som ã ʒãvje/ – It's January.

Quelle est la date du concert ?

> **C'est le 15 novembre.** /sɛ lə kẽz nɔvãbʀ/ – It's on November 15th.

> **C'est demain.** /sɛ d(ə)mẽ / – It's tomorrow.

Hier, c'était dimanche. /jɛʀ sɛtɛ dimãʃ/ – Yesterday was Sunday.

Demain, c'est mardi. /d(ə)mẽ sɛ mardi/ – Tomorrow is Tuesday.

Years, Months, Seasons

le mois /lə mwa/ – month

l'an /l'année /lã – lane/ – year

cette année /sɛt ane/ – this year

l'année dernière /lane dɛʀnjer/ – last year

Il y a un ans. /ilya œ☐ ☐☐/ – one year ago

Il y a deux ans /ilya døz ã/ – two years ago

l'année prochaine /lane pʀɔʃɛ̃/ – next year

dans deux ans /dã dø ã/– in two years

l'année prochaine /lane pʀɔʃɛ̃/ – next year

l'année dernière /lane dɛʀnje/ – last year

toute l'année /tut lane/ – all year long

chaque année /ʃak ane/ – every year

la décennie /la deseni/ – decade

le siècle /lə sjɛkl/ – century

Seasons

le printemps /pʀɛ̃tã/ – spring

l'été (m.) /ete/ – summer

l'automne (m.) /ɔtɔn/ ––fall

l'hiver (m.) /ivɛʀ/ – winter

Months

janvier /ʒãvje/ – January

février /fevʀije/ – February

mars /maʀs/ – March

avril /avʀil/ – April

mai /mɛ/ – May

juin /ʒɥɛ̃/ – June

juillet /ʒɥijɛ/ – July

août /u(t)/ – August

septembre /sɛp'tɛmbəʀ/ – September

octobre /ɔktɔbʀ/ – October

novembre /nɔvãbʀ/ – November

décembre /desãbʀ/ – December

Common Phrases

en juillet /ã ʒɥijɛ/ – in july

jusqu'en février /ʒyskã fevʀije/ – until february

à partir de novembre /a partir d nɔvãbʀ/ – from November

il y a un mois /ilja œ☐ mwa/ – a month ago

dans un mois /dã œ☐ mwa/ – in a month

ce mois–ci /sə mwa si/ – this month

le mois prochain /lə mwa pʀɔʃɛ̃/ – next month

What Time is it ?

la seconde /la s(ə)gɔ̃d/ – second

l'heure /lœʀ/ – hour

la minute /minyt/ – minute

There are three French translations for "time," each with a different meaning but with very distinct nuances and uses.

Heure – refers to clock time.

Quelle heure est–il ? – What time is it?

Temps – means either time or weather.

Ils ont le temps de faire la fête. – They have time to celebrate.

Fois – used to refer to one or several instances of an event.

J'ai appelé Pierre quatre fois aujourd'hui ! – I called Pierre 4 times today!

Quelle heure est–il ? – What time is it?

In French, the time is expressed that way: first you tell the round hour, and then the half hour, quarter or number of minutes until 30. For the time between half an hour and the full hour, you express the number of minutes remaining until the full hour.

1h00 – Il est une heure. */il ε yn œʀ/* – It's 1AM.

2h00 – Il est deux heures. */il ε døz œʀ/* – It's 2AM.

3h15 – Il est trois heures et quart. */il ε tʀwaz œʀ e kaʀ/* – It's 3:15AM.

4h30 – Il est quatre heures et demie. */il ε katʀ œʀ e demi/* – It's 4:30AM.

4h45 – Il est cinq heures moins le quart. */il ε sε□k œʀ mwε□ lə kar/* – It's 4:45AM.

or Il est quatre heures quarante–cinq. */il ε katʀ œʀ kaʀa□t sε□k/*

5h20 – Il est cinq heures vingt. */il ε sε□k œʀ vε□/* – It's 5:20AM.

8h40 – Il est neuf heures moins vingt. */il ε nœv œʀ mwε□ vε□/* – It's 8:40AM.

Useful Sentences

Je suis parti ce matin. */ʒə sɥi parti sə matε□/* – I left this morning.

Je travaille toute la journée. /ʒə tʀavaje tut la ʒuʀne/ – I work all day.

Il y a une réunion ce soir. /ilja yn ʀeynjɔ□ sə swar/ – There's a meeting this evening.

J'ai un rendez–vous demain. /ʒɛ œ□ ʀa□devu d(ə)mɛ□/ – I have a meeting tomorrow.

Il y a trois ans que j'ai voyagé en France. /ilja tʀwaza□ kə ʒɛ vwajaʒ a□ fʀa□s/ – It has been 3 years that I traveled to France.

Je serai absent à partir du seize décembre. /ʒɛ absen a partir dy sɛz desa□bʀ/ – I will be absent starting December 16th.

On arrive le cinq septembre. /ɔ□ ariv lə sɛ□k sɛpta□bʀ/ – We arrive on September 5th.

Nous parlons depuis une heure. /nu parlon dəpчi yn œʀ/ – We've been talking for an hour.

Il va parler pendant une heure. /il va parle pa□da□ yn œʀ/ – He's going to speak for an hour.

Nous mangerons dans 10 minutes. /nu ma□ʒeron da□ diminyt/ – We'll eat in 10 minutes.

Retrouvons–nous à 10 heures. /ʀətʀuvon nu a diz œʀ/ – Let's meet at 10 o'clock.

Le bus part à 7 heures. /lə bys par a setœʀ/ – The bus leaves at 7 o'clock.

Chapter 7: Weather

L'important c'est d'avoir le soleil à l'intérieur. Les nuages sont toujours passagers de toute façon.

Arisko D'Amour

The French are rumored to hate small talk. This isn't entirely true, since small talk is fine with strangers or vague acquaintances. You may meet a neighbor occasionally on the staircase whose name you don't know and it's completely okay if you begin talking about the weather. In general, older generations tend to be more accepting of small talk than younger generations who may find it shallow or fake.

There's one verb you need if you want to talk about the weather in French. It is *"faire"* or more specifically, the impersonal *"il fait"*. The French will ask *"**Quel temps fait–il ?**"* or "What's the weather like?". Remember that you can't use the verb *"être"* (to be), you need either *"faire"* or a specific verb like *"pleuvoir"* (to rain).

Vocabulary

la pluie */la plyi/–* rain

le soleil */lə sɔlɛj/* – sun

le tonnerre */lə tɔnɛʀ/* – thunder

l'orage */lɔʀaʒ/–* thunderstorm

l'ouragan */luʀagã/* – hurricane

la tempête */tãpɛt/* – storm

l'éclair /leklɛʀ/ – lightning

la température /tãpeʀatyʀ/ – temperature

le nuage /nɥaʒ/ – cloud

la glace /glas/ – ice

l'arc–en–ciel /laʀkãsjɛl/ – rainbow

le tremblement de terre /lə tʀãbləmã də tɛʀ/ – earthquake

l'inondation /linõdasjõ/ – flood

What's the weather like?

Let's take a look at different ways to respond or simply talk about the weather.

Il fait + adjective /il fɛ/ – It's (used to describe the most basic weather states)

Il fait beau. /il fɛ bo/ – It's nice.

Il fait chaud. /il fɛ ʃo/ – It's hot.

Il fait froid. /il fɛ fʀwa/ – It's cold.

Il fait frais. /il fɛ fʀɛ/ – It's fresh.

Il fait humide. /il fɛ hjuːmɪd/ – It's humide.

Il fait lourd. /il fɛ luʀ/ – It's heavy.

Il fait nuageux. /il fɛ nɥaʒø/ – It's cloudy.

Il fait orageux. /il fɛ ɔʀaʒø/ – It's stormy.

Il fait mauvais. /il fɛ mɔvɛ/ – bad weather

or **C'est + adjective** (nuageux/orageux/ pluvieux) – It's cloudy/stormy/rainy.

Il y a + noun /il ja/ – There is

Il y a du soleil /dy sɔlɛj/ – It's sunny.

83

Il y a du vent /dy vã/ – It's windy.

Il y a du brouillard /dy bʀujaʀ/ – It's foggy.

Il y a de l'orage. – There's a storm.

Il y a de la tempête. – There's a storm.

Il + verb – It's (used mostly when the sky is pouring something on you)

Il pleut. /il plø/ – It's raining.

Il pleut à verse. /il plø a vers/ – It's pouring rain.

Il neige. /il nɛʒ/ – It's snowing.

Il gèle. /il ʒɛl/ – It's freezing.

If you wish to put more intensity and say that the weather is very cold, humid or hot, you can always place the adverbs *"très"* or *"beaucoup"* in front of a noun.

Beaucoup /boku/ – a lot, much

Très /tʀɛ/ – very

Il fait très beau. /il fɛ tʀɛ bo/ – The weather is very nice.

Il y a beaucoup de vent. /ilja boku də vã/ – It's very windy.

Quel temps fait–il ? /kɛl tã fɛtil/ – What's the weather like?

> **Il pleut.** /il plø/ – It's raining.

Quel temps est prévu pour aujourd'hui ? /kɛl tã ɛ prevy pur oʒuʀdɥi/ – What's the weather forecast for today?

Quel temps est prévu pour cette semaine ? /kɛl tã ɛ prevy pur set s(ə)mɛn/ – What's the weather forecast for this week?

> **Il fera orageux cette semaine.** /il fera ɔʀaʒø set s(ə)mɛn /– It's going to be stormy this week.

À partir de vendredi, le beau temps revient. /a partir də vãdrədi lə bo tã ʀ(ə)vjẽ/ – From Friday, the good weather returns.

Il fera quel temps demain ? /il fera kɛl tã d(ə)mẽ/ – What will be the weather like tomorrow?

Il fera froid demain. /il fera frwa d(ə)mẽ/ – It's going to be cold tomorrow.

Demain, il va pleuvoir. /d(ə)mẽ il va pløvwaʀ/ – It's going to rain tomorrow.

Il fait quelle température ? /il fɛ kɛl tãperatyʀ/ – What is the temperature?

Il fait 25 degrés. /il fɛ vẽ sẽk degre/ – It's 25 degrees.

Il fait moins deux degrés. /il fɛ mwa dø degre/ – It's minus two.

Va-t-il neiger ? /vatil neʒe/ – Is it going to snow?

Fait-il nuageux ? /fɛtil nɥaʒø/ – Is it cloudy?

Common Phrases

Le brouillard se lève. /lə bʀujaʀ sə lɛv/ – The fog is lifting.

Il y a eu du soleil toute la journée ! /il y a y dy sɔlɛj tut la ʒuʀne/ – It was sunny all day long!

Il fait un temps magnifique. /il f□t œ□ t□□ ma□ifik/ – It's a gorgeous day.

Le temps s'ameliore. /lə tã sameljɔʀ/ – The weather is getting better.

Le temps se dégrade. /lə tã sə degʀad/ – The weather is getting worse.

Il y a un soleil radieux. /ilya œ□ s□l□j □adjø/ – The sun is very bright.

Quel beau lever de soleil ! /kɛl bo leve də sɔlɛj/ – What a beautiful sunrise!

Quel beau coucher de soleil ! /kɛl bo kuʃe də sɔlɛj/ – What a beautiful sunset!

Il pleut des cordes. /il plø de kɔʀd/ – It's raining cats and dogs.

Il est tombé quelques gouttes. /il e tombe kɛlk gut/ – We got a few drops of rain.

Il fait un temps affreux. /il f☐t œ☐ t☐☐ af☐ø/ – The weather is awful.

Le ciel est couvert. /lə sjɛl e kuvɛʀ/ – The sky is overcast.

C'est la canicule. /sɛ la kanikyl/ – It's a heat wave.

D'après la météo, il fera beau. /dapʀɛ la meteo il fera bo/ – According to the weather forecast, the weather will be nice.

Il pleut toujours beaucoup en mai. /il plø tuʒuʀ boku ã mɛ/ – It always rains a lot in May.

Chapter 8: Traveling

Rester, c'est exister. Voyager, c'est vivre.

Gustave Nadaud

There's one French word you should know as a tourist: the word "*visiter*". Although similar to the English word, it means "to take" or "to go on a tour". You'll see it's everywhere you look.

In a City

le plan de la ville /lə plæn de la vil/ – city map

le centre /lə sãtʀ/ – city center

la banlieue /la bãljø/ – suburbs

la rue /la ʀy/ – street

l'avenue (f.) /lə av(ə)ny/ – avenue

le pont /lə pɔ̃/ – bridge

la place /la plas/ – square

le jardin public /lə ʒaʀdɛ̃ pyblik/ – public garden

le stade /lə stad/ – stadium

le marché /lə maʀʃe/ – market

le marché aux puces /lə maʀʃe opys/ – flea market

la foire /la fwaʀ/ – fair

l'usine (f.) /lyzin/ – factory

le cinéma /lə sinema/ – movies

le théâtre /lə teatʀ/ – theatre

la poste /la pɔst/ – post office

l'agence de voyages (f.) /laʒãs də vwajaʒ/ – travel agency

la police /lə pɔlis/ – police

le parc /lə park/ – *parc*

l'hôtel de la ville (m.) /lɔtɛl də la vil/ – city hall

la mairie /la meri/ – town hall

le palais /lə palɛ/ – palace

le château /lə ʃato/ – castle

la cathédrale /la katedʀal/ – cathedral

l'église /legliz/ – church

la tour /la tuʀ/ – tower

le monument /lə mɔnymã – monument

l'exposition (f.) /lɛkspozisjɔ̃/ – exhibition

le cimetière /lə simtjɛʀ/ – cemetery

les ruines (f.) /le ʀɥin/ – ruin

le musée /lə myze/ – museum

la bibliotheque /la biblijɔtɛk/ – library

le port /lə pɔʀ/ – harbor

le jardin /lə ʒaʀdɛ̃/ – garden

le monastère /lə mɔnastɛʀ/ – monastery

la salle de concert /la sal d kɔ̃sɛʀ/ – concert hall

Sightseeing

le tourisme /lə tuʀism/ – sightseeing

l'attraction touristique (f.) /latʀaksjɔ̃ turistik/– tourist attraction

faire la visite /fɛʀ la vizit/ – to do the tour

le touriste /lə tuʀɪst/ – tourist

le guide /lə gid/ – guide book AND tour guide

la visite guidée /la vizit gide/ – guided tour

l'itinéraire (m.) /litineʀɛʀ/ – itinerary

acheter un souvenir /a□(□)te œ□ suv□ni□/ – to buy a souvenir

les attractions (f.) /lezatʀaksjɔ̃/ – attractions

le prix d'entrée /lə pri ɑ̃tʀe/ – entrance fee/price

ouvert /uvɛʀ/– open

fermé /fɛʀme/ – closed

Common Phrases

Qu'y a-t-il à voir dans cette ville ? /kjatil a vwaʀ dɑ̃ sɛt vil/ – What is there to see in this city?

Vous recommandez quels monuments locaux ? /vu ʀəkɔmɑ̃de kɛl mɔnymɑ̃ loko/ – What local monuments do you recommend visiting?

Où est-ce qu'on peut avoir des informations sur la ville ? /u ɛsk ɔ̃ pø avwaʀ dezɛ̃fɔrmasjɔ̃ syʀ la vil /– Where can we get information about the city?

C'est combien le plan de la ville ? /sɛ kɔ̃bjɛ̃ lə plɑ̃ də la vil/ – How much is the city map ?

Vous avez aussi un guide en anglais ? /vuzave osi œ□ gid □□ □□□l□/ – Do you also have an English guide?

On aimerait visiter la ville. /ɔ̃ emrɛ vizite la vil/ – We would like to visit the city.

On aimerait réserver une visite guidée. /ɔ̃ emrɛ rezervɛ yn vizit gide/– We would like to book a guided tour.

On aimerait réserver un circuit. /ɔ̃ emrɛ rezervɛ œ☐ siʀkɥi/ – We would like to book a tour.

Combien de temps dure la visite ? /kɔ̃bjɛ̃ də tɑ̃ dyr la vizit/ – How long is the visit?

Il y a un parc près d'ici ? /ilja œ☐ park prɛ disi/ – Is there a park nearby?

Vous pouvez nous faire visiter la ville ? /vu puve nu promene dɑ̃ la vil/ – Can you take us around the city?

C'est quoi ce bâtiment/monument ? /sɛ kwa sə batimɑ̃/mɔnymɑ̃/ – What is this building/monument?

Quand est-ce que cette cathédrale a été bâtie ? /kɑ̃ ɛsk sɛt katedʀal a ete bati/ – When was this cathedral built?

Qui est l'architecte ? /ki ɛ laʀʃitɛkt/ – Who's the architect?

Quel est cet édifice ? /kɛl e sɛt edifis/– What is this building?

On peut aller voir à l'intérieur ? /ɔ̃ pø ale vwa☐ al ☐☐te☐jœ☐/ – Can we go inside?

Je peux prendre des photos ici ? /ʒə pø pʀɑ̃dʀ de fɔto isi/ – Can I take pictures here?

Il y a des toilettes publiques par ici ? /ilja de twalɛt pyblik par isi/ – Are there public toilets around here?

Est-ce que je peux acheter des cartes postales / souvenirs ici ? /ɛsk ʒə pø aʃəte de kart postal isi / suvenir/ – Can I buy postcards / souvenirs here?

Purchasing Tickets

Où est-ce qu'on achète les billets ? /u esk ɔ̃ aʃət le bijɛ/ – Where do we buy the tickets?

L'entrée est payante ? /lɑ̃tre e pɛjɑ̃/ – Is there an entrance fee?

Combien coûte le billet d'entrée ? /kɔ̃bjɛ̃ kute lə bijɛ dɑ̃tʀe/ – How much does the entrance ticket cost?

Quand le musée est-il ouvert ? /kɑ̃ lə myze etil uvɛʀ/ – When is the museum open?

> **Ouvert toute la journée.** /uvɛʀ tut la ʒuʀne/ – Open all day.

À quelle heure l'église ferme-t-elle ? /a kɛl œ☐ le☐liz f☐☐m tel/ – What time does the church close?

In Nature

l'arbre (m.) /laʀbʀ/ – tree

la fleur /la flœ☐/ – flower

l'herbe (m.) /lɛʀb/ – grass

le ciel /lə sjɛl/ – sky

le vent /lə vɑ̃/ – wind

le nuage /lə nɥaʒ/ – cloud

la campagne /la kɑ̃paɲ/ – countryside

le paysage /peizaʒ/ – landscape/scenery

la forêt /la fɔʀɛ/ – forest

la terre /la tɛʀ/ – ground/earth

la colline /la kɔlin/ – hill

la montagne /la mɔ̃taɲ/ – mountain

la falaise /la falɛz/ – cliff

la vallée /la vale/ – valley

la plage /la plaʒ/ – beach

le désert /lə dezɛʀ/ – desert

la prairie /la pʀeʀi/ – meadow

la jungle /la □œ□□l/ – jungle

le chemin /lə ʃəmɛ̃/ – path

la côte, le littoral /la kɔt/ /lə litɔʀal/ – coast

l'île (f.) /lil/ – island

Bodies of Water

le lac /lə lak/ – lake

la mare or le bassin /la maʀ/ /lə basɛ̃/ – pond

la source thermale /la suʀs tɛʀmal/ – thermal source

la chute d'eau /la ʃyt do / – waterfall

le fleuve or la rivière /lə flœv/ /la ʀivjɛʀ/ – river

la mer /la mɛʀ/ – sea

l'ocean (m.) /lɔseã/ – ocean

Hiking and Mountain Climbing

la balade / la promenade /la balad/ /la pʀɔmənad/ – leisure walk

la randonnée /la ʀɑ̃dɔne/ – hike

le randonneur, la randonneuse /la □□□d□nœ□/ /lə □□□d□nœz/ – hiker

randonner /ʀɑ̃dɔne/ – to hike

l'itinéraire (m.) /litineʀɛʀ/ – route

le panneau /lə pano/ – sign

l'ascension (f.) /asãsjɔ̃/ – ascent

le point de départ /lə pwɛ̃ də depaʀ/ – starting point

l'aller–retour (m.) /lale ʀətuʀ/ – round trip

la cabane /la kaban/ – wooden house

le refuge /lə ʀəfyʒ/ – shelter

le pique–nique /lə piknik/ – picnic

le belvédère /lə bɛlvedɛʀ/ – viewpoint

la carte /la kaʀt/ – map

Equipment

le sac à dos /lə sak ado/ – backpack

des chaussures de randonnée (f.) /de ʃosyʀ də ʀãdɔne/ – hiking shoes

la combinaison de ski /la kɔ̃binɛzɔ̃ də ski/ – ski suit

l'anorak (m.) /lanorak/ – ski jacket

Common Phrases

Vous organisez des excursions ? /vuzorganize dezɛkskyʀsjɔ̃/ – Do you organize excursions?

On aimerait réserver une promenade. /ɔ̃ ɛmʀɛ ʀezɛʀve yn pʀɔmənad/ – We'd like to book a ride.

On voudrait faire une excursion dans les environs. /ɔ̃ vudʀɛ fɛʀ yn ɛkskyʀsjɔ̃ dã lez ãviʀɔ̃/ – We would like to make an excursion in the surroundings.

Combien de temps prend la randonnée ? /kɔ̃bjɛ̃ də tã pʀãd la ʀãdɔne/ – How long does the hike take?

Combien coûte une telle excursion ? /kɔ̃bjɛ̃ kut yn tɛl ɛkskyʀsjɔ̃/ – How much does such an excursion cost?

Je voudrais commander une excursion d'une journée pour quatre personnes.

/ʒə vudʀɛ kɔmɑ̃de yn ɛkskyʀsjɔ̃ dynə ʒuʀne puʀ katʀ pɛʀsɔn/ – I would like to order an all day tour for four people.

On aimerait faire une randonnée d'une journée ? / ɔ̃ ɛmʀɛ fɛʀ yn ʀɑ̃dɔne dynə ʒuʀne / – We would like to go on an all–day hike ?

On aimerait aller voir les chutes d'eau. /ɔ̃ ɛmʀɛ ale vwaʀ le ʃyt do/ – We would like to see the waterfalls.

Il y a un endroit avec une belle vue ? /ilja œ□ □□d□wa av□k yn bɛl vy/ – Is there a place with a nice view?

Quel est le nom de cette montagne–là ? /kɛl e lə nɔ̃ də sɛt mɔ̃taɲ la/ – What is the name of that mountain?

Ça prend combien de temps pour y aller à pied ? /sa pʀɑ̃d kɔ̃bjɛ̃ də tɑ̃ puʀ iale apje/ – How long does it take to walk there?

C'est combien de kilomètres ? /se kɔ̃bjɛ̃ də kilɔmɛtʀ/ – How many kilometers is it?

Qu'est ce qu'il faut prendre ? /kɛskil fo pʀɑ̃d/ – What should we take?

Quel est le chemin le plus court pour monter cette colline–là ? /kɛl e lə ʃəmɛ̃ lə ply kuʀ puʀ monte sɛt kolin la/ – What is the shortest way to climb that hill?

On pourrait essayer de monter sur cette colline ? /ɔ̃ puʀɛ eseje də monte syʀ sɛt kolin/ – Could we try to climb this hill?

C'est accessible en voiture ? /se aksesibl ɑ̃ vwatyʀ/ – Is it accessible by car?

Je suis assez fatigué. /ʒə sɥi ase fatige/ – I am quite tired.

On peut se baigner dans le lac ? /ɔ̃ pø sə beɲe dã lə lak/ – Can we swim in the lake?

Est-ce que l'eau est potable ? /ɛsk lo e potabl/ – Is the water drinkable?

On pourrait se reposer un peu ? /□□ pur□ s□ □□poze œ□ pø/ – Could we rest a bit?

Est–ce que c'est raide ? /ɛsk sɛ rɛdə / – Is it steep?

Je rentre. /ʒə ʀɑ̃tʀ / – I go home.

Camping

le terrain de camping /l□ te□□□ d□ k□□piŋ/ – camping site

la batterie /la batʀi/ – battery

la lampe de poche /la lamp də pɔʃ/ – flashlight

le matelas pneumatique /lə matəla pnømatik/ – air mattress

le réfrigérateur /lə □ef□i□e□atœ□/ – refrigerator

la poubelle /la pubɛl/ – garbage can

la pelle /la pɛl/ – shovel

le déchet /lə deʃɛ/ – waste

l'eau potable /lo potabl/ – drinking water

le réchaud à gaz / à alcool /lə ʀeʃo a gaz / alkɔl/ – gas/alcohol stove

les allumettes (f.) /lezalymɛt/ – match

la bouteille isolante /la butɛj izolant/ – insulating bottle

l'eau chaude /lo ʃod/ – warm water

la douche /la duʃ/ – shower

Common Phrases

Est-ce que vous avez encore de la place ? /ɛsk vuzave ãkɔʀ də la plas/ – Do you still have room?

Nous restons trois jours. /nu ʀɛsto trwa ʒuʀ/ – We are staying for 3 days.

Combien ça coûte ? /kɔ̃bjɛ̃ pɛjt ɔ̃/ – How much is it?

>**Par jour et par personne** /par ʒuʀ e par pɛʀsɔn/ – per day and per person

>**Pour la tente** /puʀ la tãt/ – for the tent

>**Pour la voiture** /puʀ la vwatyʀ/ – for the car

Est-ce que vous louez des caravanes ? /ɛsk vu lwe de kaʀavan/ – Do you rent caravans?

J'ai besoin de la connexion électrique. /ʒɛ bəzwɛ̃ də la kɔnɛksjɔ̃ elɛktʀik/ – I need the electrical connection.

Où puis-je changer/remplir/prendre en location la bouteille de gaz ? /u pɥi ʒə ʃãʒe/ʀãpliʀ/pʀãdʀ ã lɔkasjɔ̃ la butɛj d gaz/ – Where can I change/fill/rent the gas bottle?

On the Beach

la piscine /la pisin/ – swimming pool

le sable /lə sabl/ – sand

la plage /la plaʒ/ – beach

le bain de soleil /bɛ̃ də sɔlɛj/ – sunbathing

la crème solaire /la crem sɔlɛʀ/ – sunscreen

la douche /la duʃ/ – shower

le maillot de bain /le majo d bɛ̃/ – swimming suit

la méduse /la medyz/ – jellyfish

l'oursin (m.) /uʀsɛ̃/ – sea urchin

l'insolation (f.) /ɛ̃sɔlasjɔ̃/ – sunstroke

Common Phrases

Baignade interdite ! /bɛɲad ɛ□tɛʀdi/ – Swimming is forbidden!

L'eau ici est-elle profonde ? – Is the water here deep?

Peut-on prendre un bain ici ? – Can we take a bath here?

Je desire louer – I want to rent

Une cabane /yn kaban/ – shed

Un parasol /paʀasɔl/ – umbrella

Une chaise–longue /yn ʃɛz lɔ□g/ – deckchair

Des skis nautiques /de ski notik/ – water skis

Chapter 9: Accomodation

Le monde est un livre et ceux qui ne voyagent pas n'en lisent qu'une page.

Saint Augustin

As a tourist, you can choose between hotels, hostels, airbnb, or even camping sites. If you are coming as a student, finding student housing can be much cheaper. We recommend you search for student residences first, like CROUS, because they are significantly cheaper than private housing. You can expect fierce competition, especially in larger cities like Paris, Bordeaux, or Lyon.

la réception / *la ʀesɛpsjɔ̃* / – reception

la cuisine / *la kɥizin* / – kitchen

l'ascenseur (m.) / *las☐☐sœ☐* / – lift

hors saison / *ɔʀ sɛzɔ̃* / – off season

la saison d'été / *la sɛzɔ̃ dete* / – summer season

la saison d'hiver / *la sɛzɔ̃ diver* / – winter season

la taxe de séjour / *la taks d seʒuʀ* / – tourist tax

le propriétaire / *pʀɔpʀijetɛʀ* / – owner

le garçon / *l ɡaʀsɔ̃* / – waiter

la serveuse / *la sɛʀv* / – waitress

le cuisinier / *kɥizine* / – cook

le concierge / *kɔ̃sjɛʀʒ* / – concierge

le porteur / p☐☐tœ☐ / – carrier

la femme de chambre / fam də ʃɑ̃bʀ / – maid

Making a Reservation

J'ai réservé une chambre au nom de (). /ʒɛ rezerve yn ʃɑ̃bʀ o nɔ̃ də/ – I booked a room under the name of ().

Avez-vous des chambres libres pour (la date) ? /ave vu de ʃɑ̃bʀ libr pur/ – Do you have free rooms for (date)?

Quel type de chambre souhaitez-vous ? /kɛl tip d ʃɑ̃bʀ swetevu/ – What kind of room do you want?

> **Je voudrais réserver une chambre () pour (number of days)** /ʒə vudrɛ rezerve yn ʃɑ̃bʀ pur ()/ – I would like to book a () room for (number of days).

>> **une chambre individuelle** /yn ʃɑ̃bʀ ɛ̃dividɥɛl/ – a single room

>> **une chambre double** / yn ʃɑ̃bʀ dubl/ – a double room

>> **avec salle de bains** /avɛk sal d bɛ̃/ – with bathroom

>> **avec balcon** /avɛk balkɔ̃/ – with balcony

>> **avec petit déjeuner** /av☐k p☐ti de☐œne/ – with breakfast

> **Je voudrais** /ʒə vudrɛ/ – I would like

>> **une pension complète** /yn pɑ̃sjɔ̃ kɔ̃plɛ/ – full board (breakfast, lunch and diner)

>> **demi–pension** /yn demi pɑ̃sjɔ̃/ – half board (breakfast and diner)

Combien de temps comptez–vous rester ? /kɔ̃bjɛ̃ də tɑ̃ kɔ̃te vu ʀɛste/ – How long do you intend to stay?

Je resterai /ʒə restɛrɛ/ – I'll stay

- **une nuit** /yn nɥi/ – one night
- **(X) jours** / ʒuʀ / – days
- **deux semaines** /dø səmɛn/ – two weeks

Pricing

C'est combien une chambre double pour une nuit ? /sɛ kɔ̃bjɛ̃ yn ʃãbʀ dubl puʀ yn nɥi/ – How much is a double room for one night?

On paie d'avance ou au départ ? /ɔ̃ pɛj davãs u o depaʀ/ – Do we pay in advance or on departure?

Je veux annuler la réservation au nom de (name). /ʒə vø anule la ʀɛzɛʀvasjɔ̃ o nɔ̃ de/ – I want to cancel the reservation under the name of ().

Vous facturez des frais d'annulation ? /vu faktuʀe de fʀɛ danylasjɔ̃/ – Do you charge cancellation fees?

Combien de temps à l'avance est-ce que je peux annuler la réservation sans frais ? /kɔ̃bjɛ̃ də tã alavãs esk ʒə pø anule la ʀɛzɛʀvasjɔ̃ sã fʀɛ/ – How far in advance can I cancel the reservation free of charge?

La caution sera remboursée ? /la kosjɔ̃ sera ʀãbuʀse/ – Will the deposit be refunded?

Ce montant est-il remboursable ? /sə mɔ̃tã etil ʀãbuʀsabl/ – Is this amount refundable?

Le petit déjeuner est–il inclus ? /l☐ de☐œne ☐til ☐☐kly/ – Is breakfast included?

Arrival

Quel est le numéro de ma chambre ? /kɛl ɛ lə numero də ma ʃɑ̃bʀ/
– What is my room number?

Pourriez-vous me montrer ma chambre ? /puʀije vu mə mɔ̃tʀe ma ʃɑ̃bʀ/ – Could you show me my room?

Complaints

Cette chambre ne me convient pas. /sɛt ʃɑ̃bʀ nə mə kɔ̃vnjɑ̃ pa/ – This room does not suit me.

La chambre est trop petite. /la ʃɑ̃bʀ ɛ tro pəti/ – This room is too small.

Il n'y a pas d'eau chaude. /ilnija pa do ʃo/ – There is no hot water.

Le chauffage ne marche pas. /lə ʃofaʒ n maʀʃ pa/ – The heating does not work.

Je voudrais une autre chambre. /ʒə vudrɛ yn otr ʃɑ̃bʀ/ – I would like another room.

J'ai perdu la clé de ma chambre. /ʒɛ perdy la kle də ma ʃɑ̃bʀ/ – I've lost my room key.

In a hotel

On peut garer la voiture ici ? /ɔ̃ pø gare la vwatyʀ isi/ – Can we park the car here?

On peut avoir des serviettes propres, s'il vous plaît ? /ɔ̃ pø avwar de sɛʀvjɛt propr sil vu plɛ/ – Can we have clean towels, please?

On sert le petit déjeuner/dîner à quelle heure ? /ɔ̃ ser lə pəti de□œne/ dine a k□l œ□/ – What time is breakfast/dinner served?

Donnez–moi la clef de ma chambre, s'il vous plaît. /*done mwa la kle də ma ʃɑ̃bʀ sil vu plɛ*/ – Give me my room key, please.

Je voudrais avoir /*ʒə vudʀɛ avwaʀ*/ – I would like to get.

    Un oreiller /*œ□ □□eje*/ – a pillow

Une couverture /*yn kuvɛʀtyʀ*/ – cover

Departure

Il faut libérer la chambre avant quelle heure ? /*il fo libere la ʃa□bʀ ava□ kɛl œʀ*/ – What time the room should be vacated ?

Je pars demain matin à huit heures. /*ʒə par dəmɛ□ matɛ□ a ɥi(t) œʀ*/ – I am leaving tomorrow morning at eight o'clock.

Appelez–moi un taxi, s'il vous plaît. /*apəle mwa œ□ taksi sil vu plɛ*/ – Call me a taxi, please.

Je veux régler la note. /*ʒə vø regle la not*/ – I want to pay the bill.

Chapter 10: Culture and Entertainment

Toute culture naît du mélange, de la rencontre, des chocs.
A l'inverse, c'est de l'isolement que meurent les civilisations.

Octavio Paz

French culture is reflected in every building, palace, monument or even street, but the finest examples of French culture can be found in museums. A visit to France would not be complete without visiting one of its museums. However, prepare for long queuing in front of the most famous museums like the *Louvre* or *Orsay*. There are 1218 museums in France, so you're sure to find one you'll enjoy without having to wait in line. All museums are free to enter on the first Sunday of every month throughout France. There's also a discount price *"tarif reduit"* for students and seniors.

Cinema, Theater, Concert

le prix d'entrée /lə pri dɑ̃tʀe/ – entrance fee

le prix adulte /lə pri adylt/ – adult price

le tarif réduit /lə taʀif ʀedɥi/ – reduced rate

le tarif /lə taʀif/ – price

      étudiant /etydjɑ̃/ – student

      enfant /ɑ̃fɑ̃/ – child

de groupe /də grup/ – group rate

complet /kɔ̃plɛ/ – full

l'entrée libre /lɑ̃tre libr/ – free entrance

le concert /lə kɔnser/ – concert

le chanteur /lə □□□tœ□/ – singer (m.)

la chanteuse /la □□□tœz/ – singer, (f.)

le groupe de musique /lə grup də muzik/ – music group

le théâtre /lə teatr/ – theatre

le théâtre de marionnettes /lə teatr də marjɔnɛt/ – puppet theater

le spectacle, la pièce de théâtre /lə spɛktakl/ /la pjɛs də teatr/ – drama, play

le thétre contemporain /lə teatr kɔ̃tɑ̃pɔrɛ̃/ – modern theater

    la comédie /la kɔmedi/ – comedy

    la tragédie /la traʒedi/ – tragedy

    l'opéra (m.) /lopera/ – opera

    le ballet /lə balɛ/ – ballet

le cinéma /le kɔmedi/ – movie theater

    le film d'action /lə film daksjɔ̃/ – action movie

    le film policier /lə film pɔlisje/ – police movie

    le thriller / le film à suspense /lə thriller/ /lə film a syspɑ̃s/ – thriller

    le film d'horreur /lə film □□œ□/ – horror movie

    le film de guerre /lə film də gɛr/ – war movie

    le documentaire /lə dɔkymɑ̃tɛr/ – documentary

    la parodie /la parɔdi/ – parody

le film romantique /lə film ʀɔmãtik/ – romantic movie

le dessin animé /lə desɛ̃ anime/ – cartoon

le film pour enfants /lə film pur ãfã / – children's movie

Common Phrases

Est–ce que tu veux aller au cinéma ? /esk ty vø ale o sinema/ – Would you like to go to the cinema?

au théâtre /o teatʀ/ – to the theatre

au concert /o conser/ – to the concert

au musée /o myze/ – to the museum

Où est-ce que je peux acheter des billets ? /u esk □□ pœ a□□te de bijɛ/ – Where can I buy the tickets?

Je voudrais /ʒə vudʀɛ/ – I would like…

un billet pour le spectacle ce samedi. /œ□ bij□ pur l□ sp□ktakl sə samdi/ – one ticket for the show this Saturday.

Je voudrais réserver /ʒə vudʀɛ rezerve/ – I would like to reserve…

deux places. /dø plas/ – two seats

une place au premier rang. /yn plas o pʀəmje rã/ – a seat in the first row

C'est complet. /sɛ kɔ̃plɛ/ – All tickets are sold out.

Est–ce que l'entrée est libre ? /ɛsk lãtʀe e libr/ – Is entrance free?

Quel est le prix d'entrée ? /kɛl e lə pri dãtʀe/ – How much is admission?

Est-ce que vous avez un tarif réduit ? /□sk□ vuzave œ□ tarif redui/ – Do you have a discount price?

Ça commence à quelle heure ? /sa k□m□□se a k□l œ□/ – When does it start ?

105

Où sont nos places ? /u sɔ̃ no plas/ – Where are our seats?

Excusez–moi, ces places–ci sont à nous ? /ɛkskuze mwa se plas si son a nu/ – Excuse me, are these seats ours?

Ça vous a plu ? / sa vuza ply / – Did you like it?

 J'ai beaucoup aimé. /ʒɛ boku ɛme/ – I liked it a lot.

 Je n'ai pas trop aimé. / ʒə nɛ pa tro ɛme / – I didn't like it very much.

C'était assez intéressant. /sɛte ase ɛ̃teʀesɑ̃/ – It was quite interesting.

Sport

French uses either *"jouer"* or *"faire de"*, just as English uses the verbs *"to do"* or *"to play"* with certain kinds of sports.

jouer /ʒwe/ – to play

faire de /fɛʀ də/ – to do

le football /lə futbol/ – football

le volley–ball /lə vɔlɛbol/ – volleyball

le basket /lə baskɛt/ – basketball

le tennis /lə tenis/ – tennis

les arts martiaux /lézar maʀsjo/ – martial arts

la lutte /la lyt/ – wrestling

les sports de combat /le spor d comba/ – combat sports

la natation /la natasjɔ̃/ – swimming

la plongée /la plɔ̃ʒe/ – diving

la pêche /la peʃe/ – fishing

la voile /la vwa/ – sailing

le surf /lə sœ□f/ – surfing

le ski nautique /lə ski notik/ – water skiing

la luge /la lyʒ/ – sledging

le parachutisme /lə paʀaʃytism/ – parachuting

le patinage artistique /lə patinaʒ aʀtistik/ – figure skating

l'alpinisme /lalpinism/ – mountaineering

l'équitation /ekitasjɔ̃/ – horseback riding

la dance /la dans/ – dancing

la marche /la maʀʃ/ – walking

la musculation /la myskylasjɔ̃/ – bodybuilding

la randonnée /la ʀɑ̃dɔne/ – hiking, backpacking

le cyclisme /lə siklism/ – cycling

le vélo /lə velo/ – biking

le jogging /lə d□□□iŋ/ – jogging

l'escrime /lɛskʀim/ – fencing

le yoga /lə jɔga/ – yoga

Equipement and Sport Terms

le terrain de sport /lə teʀɛ̃ də spor/ – sport field

le filet /lə filɛ/ – net

la raquette de tennis /la ʀakɛt d tenis/ – tennis racket

le public /lə pyblik/ – the crowd

le vainqueur /lə v□□kœ□/ – winner

les spectateurs /le sp□ktatœ□/ – spectators

la salle de sport /la sal də spor/ – gym

l'entraîneur /l□□t□□nœ□/ – coach

Common Phrases

Il y un terrain de sport par ici ? /ilja œ□ te□□□ d□ sp□□ par isi/ – Is there a sport court here?

Je voudrais louer la cour pour une heure ? /□□ vudr□ lwe l□ ku□ pur yn œ□ / – I would like to rent the court for an hour?

Quand est-ce que la cour sera libre? /kã ɛsk lə kur sera libr/ – When will the court be free?

Combien on paye pour une heure / un mois ? /k□□bj□□ □□ p□j pur yn œ□ / œ□ mwa/ – How much do we pay for an hour?

Je pourrais jouer avec vous ? /ʒə purɛ ʒwe avɛk vu/ – Could I play with you?

J'aime faire du yoga. /ʒɛm fɛʀ dy yoga/ – I like to do yoga.

Y a–t–il une salle de sport à proximité ? /jatil yn sal də spor a pʀɔksimite/ – Is there a gym nearby?

Chapter 11: Transportation

Le plus beau voyage, c'est celui qu'on a pas encore fait.

Laick Peyron

France is a very well connected country and you'll easily find transportation from one point to another. The best way to travel between bigger cities is by train, **TER** (French Regional Train) or **TGV** (high–speed train). So far, **TGV** trains only operate in the Hauts–de–France region, or Paris–Lille–Calais. The **TER** allows you to travel within a given region of France at really low prices, starting at just 2 euros, depending on the distance. There are buses that travel between cities as an alternative to trains, but they are less frequent.

Buses are common in smaller cities. The subway is the best way to get around Paris and the tram is convenient in Bordeaux. There are bicycle counters everywhere in France, so you can get around the city and enjoy the views on a bike. You can even download an app that tells you where the nearest bike rental is.

Asking for Directions

To start a conversation with a person in the street or in a store, the first thing to say is *"Excusez–moi"* which means **"Excuse me"**, followed by *"Monsieur or Madame"*. This is a polite way to grab someone's attention and signal to them that you'd like to engage with them in a conversation. In French: **"Savez–vous où se trouve** la cathédrale Notre–Dame ?"

The word **"est"** is the present tense of the verb **"être"** conjugated in the third person singular. The same verb in the third person plural is **"sont"** and it must be used with plural words. For instance, the word *restrooms* is always used in its plural form in French **"les toilettes"** and therefore you should say: "**Où sont** les toilettes publiques ?"

Let's see different ways to ask for directions:

Où est-ce ? or C'est où ? /u es/ or /se u/ – Where is it?

Comment je fais pour y aller ? /kɔmɛnt ʒə fɛ puʀ i ale/ – How do I get there?

J'ai besoin d'aller à (). /ʒɛ bəzwɛ̃ dale a/ – I have to go to ().

Excusez–moi, où est ( ) le plus proche ? /ekskyze mwa u e lə ply pʀɔʃ/ – Excuse me, where is the nearest ().

C'est à quelle distance d'ici ? /sɛ a kɛl distãs disi/ – How far is it from here?

Vous pouvez me montrer la route pour aller à () ? /vu puve mə montre la rut pur ale a/ – Can you show me the way to go to ()?

Il y a un autre chemin pour y aller ? /ilja œ☐ ☐☐m☐☐ pur i ale/ – Is there another way to get there?

Est-ce que je peux y aller à pied ? /ɛsk ʒə pø i ale a pje/ – Can I walk there?

Il faut combien de temps pour y aller ? /il fo kɔ̃bjɛ̃ də tã pur i ale/ – How long does it take to get there?

Combien de temps est-ce que ça prend à pied ? /kɔ̃bjɛ̃ də tã esk sa pʀãdʀ a pje/ – How long does it take on foot?

This will help you confirm you are taking the right route:

C'est la bonne direction pour aller à ()? /sɛ la bon diʀɛksjɔ̃ pur ale a/ – Is this the right direction to go to ()?

C'est loin d'ici () ? /sɛ lwɛ̃ disi/ – It is far from here?

If you ask someone for directions, you may hear something like this:

à côté de /a kɔte də/ – next to

en face de /ã fas də/ – in front of

à droite de /a dʀawt də/ – on the right of

à gauche de /a goʃ də/ – on the left of

tout droit /tu dʀwa/ – straight ahead

tourner /tuʀne/ – to turn

derrière /dɛʀjɛʀ/ – behind

devant /dəvã/ – in front of

centre–ville /sãtʀ vil/ – city center

au coin de /o kwan də/ – at the corner of

au bout de /o bu də/ – at the end of

la prochaine rue /la pʀɔʃɛ̃ ʀy/ – next street

la rue suivante /la ʀy suivant/ – next street

première à droite /pʀəmje a dʀwat/ – first to the right

deuxième à gauche /døzjɛm a goʃ/ – the second to the left

Vous devez prendre /vu deve pʀãdʀ/ – You should take

　　　la rue suivante /la ʀy sɥivã/ – next street

　　　la seconde à droite /la səgɔ̃d a dʀwat/ – second on the right

　　　la première à gauche /la pʀəmje a goʃ/ – first on the left

Le musée est au coin de (). /lə myze e o kwɛ̃ də/ – The museum is on the corner of ().

La banque est au bout de cette rue. */la bank e o bu de la ry/* – The bank is at the end of this street.

Passport Control

la frontière nationale */la frɑ̃tɪəʳ nasjonal/* – national border

le contrôle des passeports */lə kɔ̃tʀol de paspɔʀ/* – passport control

le contrôle douanier */lə kɔ̃tʀol dwanje/* – border control

soumis à la douane */sumi a la dwan/* – subject to customs

le visa d'entrée */lə viza dɑ̃tʀe/* – entry visa

Votre passeport, s'il vous plaît. */votr paspɔʀ sil vu ple/* – Your passport please.

    Voici mon passeport. */vwasi mɔ̃ paspɔʀ/* – Here's my passport.

Nous serons à la frontière quand ? */nu seron ala fʀɔ̃tjɛʀ kɑ̃/* – When will we reach the border?

Avez-vous quelque chose à déclarer ? */ave vu kɛlkʃoz a deklare/* – Do you have anything to declare?

    Je n'ai rien à déclarer. */ʒə nɛ ʀjɛ̃ a deklare/* – I don't have anything to declare.

    J'ai quelque chose à déclarer. */ʒɛ kɛlk ʃoz a deklare/* – I have something to declare.

Combien de cigarettes avez-vous ? */kɔ̃bjɛ̃ də sigaʀɛt ave vu/* – How many cigarets do you have?

    Je n'ai que ... paquets de cigarettes. */ʒə nɛ k.. pakɛ d sigaʀɛt/* – I only have (number) of cigarettes.

Vous pouvez ouvrir vos bagages, s'il vous plaît ? */vu puve ouvrir vo bagaʒ sil vu ple/* – Can you open your luggage, please?

Vous devez payer des droits de douane. /vu dəve peje de drwa de dwan/ – You have to pay customs duties.

D'où venez-vous ? /du vene vu/ – Where do you come from?

Où allez-vous? /u ale vu/ – Where are you going?

> **Je suis ici de passage.** /ʒə sɥi isi də pasaʒ/ – I am here passing through.

> **Je suis ici pour le travail.** /ʒə sɥi isi pur lə tʀavaj/ – I am here for work.

> **Je suis ici pour les vacances.** /ʒə sɥi isi pur le vakans/ – I am here on holiday.

> **Je suis ici pour deux semaines.** /ʒə sɥi isi pur dø səmɛn/ – I am here for two weeks.

> **Je compte loger chez ...** /ʒə kɔ̃t lɔʒe ʃe/ – I plan to stay at...

Je voyage /ʒə vwajaʒ/ – I travel ...

> **comme touriste** /kɔm tuʀist/ – as a tourist

> **pour mes affaires** /pur mez afɛr/ – for my business

> **pour rendre une visite** /pur ʀɑ̃dʀ yn vizit/ – to pay a visit

Je voyage seul. /□□ vwaja□ sœl/ – I am traveling alone.

Nous voyageons ensemble. /nu vwajaʒ ɑ̃sɑ̃bl/ – We are traveling together.

Public transportation

la voiture /la vwatyʀ/ – car

le tram /lə tram/ – tram

le bus /lə bys/ – bus

le métro /lə metro/ – subway

l'arrêt (m.) /laʀɛ/ – station

le chauffeur, le conducteur /lə □ofœ□ / lə k□□dyktœ□/ – driver

le ticket /lə tiket/ – ticket

> **tarif réduit** /le tarif ʀedɥi/ – reduced price

> **journée** /ʒuʀne/ – daily reduced price

> **groupes** /grup/ – reduced price for a group

le composteur /k□□p□stœ□/ – person who validates tickets

valider/composter le ticket /valide – kɔ̃pɔste lə tikɛ/ – to validate the ticket

Making Inquiries

Où est la gare la plus proche ? /ue la gar la ply pʀɔʃ / – Where is the closest station?

Où se trouve la station de métro ? /u sə truv la stasjɔ̃ də metʀo/ – Where is the metro station?

Où est-ce que je peux acheter des billets ? /u esk □□ pœ a□□te de bij□/ – Where can I buy tickets?

Y a-t-il un arrêt près d'ici ? /jatil œ□a□□ p□□disi/ – Is there a stop near here?

Quel tram/bus/train va au centre ? /kɛl tʀam/bys/tʀɛ̃ va o sɑ̃tʀ/ – Which tram/bus/train goes to the center?

Est-ce qu'il y a une station de métro près d'ici ? /eskilja yn stasjon də metro pre disi/ – Is there a subway station nearby?

Quel bus va à () ? /kɛl bys va a ( )/ – Which bus goes to ( )?

Est-ce que je peux acheter des tickets auprès du conducteur / à bord ? /□sk□ □□ pœ a□□te de tik□ op□□ dy k□□dyktœ□ / a bor/ – Can I buy tickets from the driver / on board?

Où est-ce que je peux valider/composter mon ticket ? /u esk □□ pœ valide/k□□p□ste mɔ̃ tikɛ/ – Where can I validate/compost my ticket?

Purchasing Tickets

Combien coûte un billet simple/aller-retour pour ( ) ? /k□□bj□□ kut œ□a bij□ s□□pl/ale retur pur / – How much is a single/return ticket to ()?

Je voudrais acheter un billet pour ( ), s'il vous plaît. /□□ vudr□ a□□te œ□a bij□ pur ( ) sil vu pl□/ – I would like to buy a ticket to ..., please.

Deux billets simples pour... /dø bijɛ sɛ̃pl pur/ – Two tickets single for...

Un billet de deuxième/première classe. /œ□ bij□ d□ døzj□m / p□□mje kl□s/ – A second/first class ticket.

Est-ce qu'il y a des tarifs réduits pour les étudiants/enfants ? /eskilja de tarif ʁedɥi pur lezetydjã/ ãfã/ – Are there reduced rates for students/children?

Quand part le prochain train/bus pour ( ) ? /kã paʁ lə pʁɔʃɛ̃ tʁɛ̃/bys pur ()/ – When does the next train for ( ) leave?

Il faut combien de temps pour y aller ( ) ? /il fo kɔ̃bjɛ̃ d tã puri ale ( )/ – How long does it take to get there?

Je voudrais réserver une place. /ʒə vudʁɛ ʁezɛʁve yn plas/ – I would like to reserve a place.

Quelle est la correspondance la plus rapide / la moins chère pour ( ) ? /kɛl e la kɔʁɛspɔ̃dãs la ply rapid / la mwɛ̃ ʃɛʁ pur/ – What is the fastest/cheapest connection for ( )?

Compartiment non-fumeurs, s'il vous plaît ? /k□□pa□tim□□ n□□ fymœ□ sil vu pl□/ – Non–smoking compartment, please?

Est—ce que le train s'arrête à ( ) ? /ɛsk lə tʀɛ̃ saret a / – Does the train stop at ( )?

De quel quai part le train pour ( ) ? /də kɛl ke par lə tʀɛ̃ pur ( )/ – From which platform does the train for ( ) leave?

Train

Quel est le nom de l'arrêt où je dois descendre ? /kɛl e le nɔ̃ delaʀɛ u ʒə dwa desɑ̃dʀ/ – What is the name of the stop where I have to get off?

Quel est le nom de cet arrêt / cette station ? /kɛl e le nɔ̃ də sɛt aʀɛ / sɛt stasjɔ̃/ – What's the name of this stop/station?

Pouvez-vous me dire quand/où je dois descendre ? /puve vu mə dir quand/u ʒə dwa desɑ̃dʀ/ – Can you tell me when/where I should get off?

    Vous passez quatre arrêts. /vu pase qatr aʀɛ / – You pass four stations.

Il reste combien d'arrêts ? /il rest kɔ̃bjɛ̃ daʀɛ/ – How many stops are left?

C'est bien le train pour ... ? /sɛ bjɛ̃ lə tʀɛ̃ pur/ – Is this the train for...?

Je cherche le contrôleur. /□□ □□□□e l□ k□□t□olœ□/ – I'm looking for the controller.

Est—ce que cette place est occupée ? /ɛsk sɛt plas e ɔkype/ – Is this seat occupied?

Excusez—moi, c'est ma place. /ɛskuze mwa sɛ ma plas/ – Excuse me, this is my place.

Quelle est la destination de ce train ? /kɛl e la dɛstinasjɔ̃ də sə tʀɛ̃/ – What is the destination of this train?

Quel est le prochain arrêt ? /kɛl e lə pʀɔʃɛ̃ aʀɛ/ – What is the next station?

Où est le wagon–restaurant ? /u e lə vagɔ̃ ʀɛstɔʀɑ̃/ – Where is the dining car?

Voulez–vous qu'on échange les places ? /vule vu kɔ̃ eʃɑ̃ʒ le plas/ – Would you like to swap places?

Quand est-ce qu'on arrive à ( ) ? /kɑ̃ ɛskɔ̃ ariv a ( )/ – When do we get to ( )?

Où sommes–nous ? C'est quelle station ? /u sɔm nu / sɛ kɛl stasjon/ – Where are we? Which station is it?

J'ai raté ma station. /ʒɛ rate ma stasjon/ – I missed my station.

C'est le terminus. /sɛ lə tɛrminys/ – This is the terminus.

Le train a du retard. /lə tʀɛ̃ a dy ʀətaʀ/ – The train is late.

Taxi

Y a-t-il une station de taxis près d'ici ? /jatil yn stasjɔ̃ də taksi pre disi/ – Is there a taxi station near here?

Taxi ! Êtes-vous libre ? /taksi ete vu libr/ – Taxi! Are you available?

Conduisez–moi à cette adresse, s'il vous plaît. /kɔnduize mwa a set adrɛs sil vu plɛ/ – Take me to this address, please.

À l'aéroport, s'il vous plaît. /a laeʀopɔʀ sil vu plɛ/ – To the airport, please.

Pouvez–vous m'appeler un taxi, s'il vous plaît. /puve vu mapele œ□ taksi sil vu pl□/ – Could you please call me a cab.

Déposez-moi ici. /depoze mwa isi/ – Leave me here.

Pourriez-vous faire un petit tour de la ville ? /purje vu f□r œ□ pəti tur də la vil/ – Could you take a little tour of the city?

Pouvez-vous m'aider à mettre les bagages ? /puve vu mɛde a metr le bagaʒ/ – Can you help me put the luggage?

Uber Drive

Où allez-vous ? /u ale vu/ – Where are you going?

Choisir un véhicule ! /ʃwaziʀ yn veikyl/ – Choose a vehicle type!

Confirmer /kɔ̃fiʀme/ – to confirm

Confirmez votre lieu de prise en charge. /kɔ̃fiʀme votr ljø də priz ã ʃaʀʒ/ – Confirm your pickup location.

Attendez qu'un chauffeur accepte votre demande. /at□□de kœ□ □ofœ□ aks□pte votr d□m□□d/ – Wait for a driver to accept your request.

Le chauffeur va arriver dans 20 minutes. /lə □ofœ□ va arive d□□ v□□ minut/ – The driver will get in 20 minutes.

Une notification vous sera envoyée lorsque le chauffeur sera à proximité de votre lieu de prise en charge. /yn n□tifikasj□□ vu sera □□vwaje l□□sk l□ □ofœ□ sera a p□□ksimite d□ votr ljø dp□iz □□ □a□□/ – You'll get a notification when the driver is near your pick–up location.

Airplane

Booking a Ticket

Je voudrais acheter un billet d'avion pour ( ), s'il vous plaît. /□□ vudr□ a□□te œ□a bij□ davjon pur ( ) sil vu pl□/ – I would like to buy a ticket to ( ), please./

Combien coûte un billet d'avion en première classe / classe économique ? /k□□bj□□ kut œ□ bij□ davjon □□ p□□mje klas / klas ek□n□mik□/ – How much does a first class/economy class plane ticket cost?

C'est un vol direct ? /s□t œ□ vol di□□kt/ – Is it a direct flight?

C'est un vol avec escale ? /s□t œ□ vol av□k □skal/ – Is it a flight with a stopover?

Le vol est retardé (d'une heure) /le vol e retarde (dyn œ□)/ – The flight is late (one hour).

Votre vol est annulé ? /vɔtʀ vol etanyle/ – Is your flight canceled?

À quelle heure est le prochain vol pour ( ) ? /a k□l œ□ e p□□□□□ v□l pur ( )/ – What time is the next flight for ( )?

Je peux annuler mon billet / ma réservation ? /ʒə pø anyle mɔ̃ bije/ ma ʀezeʀvasjɔ̃/ – Can I cancel my ticket / my reservation?

Combien font les frais d'annulation ? /kɔ̃bjɛ̃ fon le fʀɛ danulasjon/ – How much are the cancellation fees?

In Airplane

On atterrit à quelle heure ? /ɔ̃ ateri a k□l œ□/ – What time do we land?

Je n'arrive pas à attacher ma ceinture. /ʒə naʀive pa a atafe ma sɛ̃tyʀ/ – I can't fasten my seat belt.

Ma liseuse ne marche pas. /ma lizøz nə maʀʃ pa/ – My reading light is not working.

Je dois aller aux toilettes. /ʒə dwa ale o twalɛt/ – I have to go to the toilets.

Les boissons sont comprises ? /le bwasɔ̃ sɔ̃ kompriz/ – Are drinks included?

Lost baggage

Où signaler la perte de bagages ? /u siɲale la pɛʀt də bagaʒ/ – Where to report lost luggage?

J'étais dans le vol numéro ( ). /ʒɛtɛ dã lə vol numero ( )/ – I was in the flight number ( ).

J'avais deux bagages. /ʒavɛ dø bagaʒ/ – I had two luggages.

C'était une valise rouge. /sɛtɛ yn valiz ʁuʒ/ – It was a red suitcase.

Contactez–moi à ce numéro là, s'il vous plaît. /kɔ̃takte mwa a sə numero la sil vu plɛ/ – Contact me at this number, please.

J'ai vraiment besoin de mes bagages. /ʒɛ vʁɛmã bəzwɛ̃ də me bagaʒ/ – I really need my luggages.

J'ai mon adresse dessus. /ʒɛ mɔ̃ adʁɛs dəsy/ – I have my address on it.

Combien de temps ça vous prendra de les trouver ? /kɔ̃bjɛ̃ də tã sa vu pʁãdra də le truve / – How long will it take you to find them?

Où demander l'indemnisation pour bagages perdus ? /u demande lɛ̃dɛmnsjon pur bagaʒ perdy/ – Where can I claim compensation for lost luggage?

Boat and Cruise

guichet d'embarquement /giʃɛ dãbaʁkəmã/ – boarding counter

passerelle d'embarquement /pasʁɛl dãbaʁkəmã/ – boarding bridge

Comment peut–on arriver au port des ferries ? /kɒmɛn pøt ɔ̃ arive o por de feri/ – How can we get to the ferry boat?

À quelle heure part le prochain ferry ? /a k□l œ□ par lə pʁɔʃɛ̃ feri/ – What time DOES the next feRry leave?

Quelle est la durée du voyage ? /kɛl e la dyre dy vwajaʒ/ – How long is the trip?

Le voyage dure environ une heure. /lə vwaja□ dyr □□vi□□□ yn œ□/ – The trip takes about an hour.

Quel est le prix pour une voiture et deux personnes ? /kɛl e lə pri pur yn vwatyr e dø pɛʁsɔn/ – What's the price for a car and two people?

Car

le permis de conduire /lə pɛʁmi d kɔ̃dɥiʁ/ – driving licence

le certificat d'immatriculation (carte grise) /lə sɛʁtifika imatʁikylasjɔ̃ (kart griz)/ – registration certificate

l'assurance traffic (carte verte) / lasyʁɑ̃s tʁæfik (kart vert)/ – traffic insurance

Où est-ce que je peux louer une voiture ? /u ɛskə ʒə pø lwe yn vwatyʁ/ – Where can I rent a car?

Je voudrais louer une petite voiture économique ? /ʒə vudʁɛ lwe yn pəti vwatyʁ ekɔnɔmik/ – I would like to rent a small economy car ?

Combien consomme cette voiture ? /kɔ̃bjɛ̃ kɔ̃sɔme sɛt vwatyʁ/ – How much does this car consume?

Il y a la clim ? /ilja la klim/ – Is there air conditioning?

Combien coûte la location par jour ? /kɔ̃bjɛ̃ kut la lɔkasjɔ̃ par ʒuʁ/ – How much is the rental per day?

Est–ce que l'essence est comprise ? /ɛskə lesɑ̃s e kompriz/ – Is gasoline included?

Je peux quitter le pays avec cette voiture ? /ʒə pø kite le pei avɛk sɛt vwatyʁ/ – Can I leave the country with this car?

Combien de kilomètres sont inclus dans le prix ? /kɔ̃bjɛ̃ də kilɔmɛtʁ sɔ̃ ɛ̃kly dɑ̃ lə pri/ – How many kilometres are included in the price?

Jusqu'à quand faut-il rendre la voiture ? /ʒyska kã fotil ʀɑ̃dʀ la vwatyʀ/ – Until when do l have to return the car?

Quel numéro appeler en cas d'accident/de panne/de vol ? /kɛl nymeʀo apəle ã ka daksidã /pan/vɔl/ – What number to call in case of accident/breakdown/theft?

Il me faut aussi un porte-bagages / un porte-vélos ? /il mə fo osi œ□ port ba□a□ / œ□ port velo/ – Do I also need a luggage/bike rack?

Il n'y a pas de roue de rechange. /il ni pa də ru d ʀəʃãʒ/ – There is no spare wheel.

Le pneu avant/arrière droit est usé. /lə pnø avã/aʀjeʀe dʀwa e yze/ – The right front/rear tire is worn.

C'est accessible en voiture ? /sɛ aksesibl ã vwatyʀ/ – Is it accessible by car?

Bike

Louer un vélo /lwe œ□ velo/ – rent a bike

Le point de location vélo /lə pwɛ̃ də lɔkasjɔ̃/ – bike rental point

Je voudrais me renseigner sur la location de vélos. /ʒə vudʀɛ ʀɑ̃seɲe syr la lokasjon də velo/ – I would like to inquire about bike rental.

Ce serait pour une location de deux vélos adultes avec une remorque pour enfants. /sə səʀe pur yn lokasjon də dø velo adylt avɛk yn ʀəmɔʀk pur ɑ̃fɑ̃/ – This would be for a rental of two adult bikes with a child trailer.

Je voudrais louer pour la journée. /ʒə vudʀɛ lwe pur la ʒuʀne/ – I would like to rent for a day.

Je paie maintenant ou au retour ? /ʒə pɛj mɛ̃tənã u o ʀətuʀ/ – Should I pay now or after we come back?

Chapter 12: Food and Drink

La gastronomie est l'art d'utiliser la nourriture pour créer du bonheur.

Théodore Zeldin

There is no doubt that French cuisine has a long history. However, cooking as an art form dates back to the 14th century and culminated during Louis XIV's reign. It's not just the refined taste that makes French cuisine unique but its elegant appearance as well. French people like to enjoy simple flavors, like having only cheese and wine for dinner. Eating is almost a sacred ritual in their culture. During lunch break, the park is often full of employees and students having picnics and enjoying the sunlight.

Some of the best traditional French meals are *Boeuf Bourguignon, Escargot, Cassoulet, Quiche Lorraine, Ratatouille, Pot-au-feu,* followed by desserts such as *Tarte Tatin, Macarons, Tarte au Citron, Brioche, Madelaine* and *Palmier.*

Ordering in a Restaurant

To address a waiter, you can use **garçon** (for a waiter), or simply **Monsieur** (for a waiter). To address a waitress, you'll say **mademoiselle**.

The waiter will ask you:

Vous désirez ? /*vu dezire*/ – What would you like?

Que voulez-vous boire? / *kə vule vu bwar* / – What would you like to drink?

Désirez-vous encore quelque chose ? /*dezire ãkɔʀ kɛlk ʃoz*/ – Would you like anything else?

You may ask:

Vous avez une table libre ? /*vuzave yn tabl libr*/ – Do you have a free table?

On peut se mettre ici ? /*ɔ̃ pø sə mɛtʀ isi* / – Can we sit here?

    Non, c'est pris. /*no se pri*/ – No, it is taken.

Je voudrais une table pour deux. /*ʒə vudʀɛ yn tabl pur dø*/ – I would like a table for two.

Garçon, s'il vous plaît. /*gaʀsɔ̃ sil vu plɛ*/ – Waiter, please. (when calling a waiter)

On voudrait commander. /*ɔ̃ vudʀɛ kɔmãde*/ – We would like to order.

Je voudrais commander à la carte. /*ʒə vudʀɛ kɔmãde a la kart*/ – I would like to order what's on the menu.

    La carte, s'il vous plaît. /*la kart sil vu plɛ*/ – Menu, please.

    La carte des vins /*la kart de vɛ̃*/ – wine menu

Qu'est-ce que vous recommandez ? /*kɛsk vu ʀəkɔmãde*/ – What do you recommend?

On a déjà commandé. /*ɔ̃ a deʒa kɔmãde*/ – We already ordered.

Comme entrée, je prends... /*kɔm ãtʀe ʒə pʀãd*/ – For starter, I take...

    une soupe / yn sup / – a soup

Quelle est votre spécialité ? /kɛl ɛ votr spesjalite/ – What's the speciality of the house?

Je voudrais quelque chose sans viande. /ʒə vudʀɛ kɛlk ʃoz sã vjãd/ – I would like something without meat.

Un autre café, s'il vous plaît. /yn otʀ kafe sil vu plɛ/ – Another coffee, please.

On peut avoir un autre couvert ? /□□ pø avwa□ œ□ kuv□□/ – Could we have another set of cutlery?

Il nous manque une fourchette / un couteau / une cuillère / une assiette /il nu m□□k yn fu□□□t / œ□ kuto / yn k□ij□□ / yn asjɛt/ – We are missing a fork/knife/spoon/plate/.

Bon appétit. /bɔ̃ apeti/ – Enjoy your meal.

Vous pouvez l'enlever. /vu puve lãləve/ – You can take the plates.

Complaints

Ce n'est pas ce qu'on a commandé. /sə nɛ pa skɔ̃ a kɔmãde/ – That's not what we have ordered.

Ce plat n'est pas bon. /sə pla nɛ pa bɔ̃/ – This dish isn't good.

Il y a trop de sel. /il ja tro də sel/ – It's too salty.

C'est cramé. /se krame/ – It's burned.

Paying

Ca fait combien ? /sa fɛ kɔ̃bjɛ̃/ – How much is that?

On paye séparément/ensemble. /ɔ̃ pɛ sepaʀemã/ãsãbl/ – We pay separately/together.

Je peux payer par carte ? /ʒə pø peje par kart/ – Can I pay by card?

Désolé, il me semble que vous nous faites payer trop cher ?
/dezɔle il m sãble kə vu nu fɛt peje tro ʃɛʀ/ – Excuse me, it looks like we have been overcharged.

On n'a pas eu ça. /ɔ̃ na pa y sa/ – We didn't get that.

C'est bon. Gardez la monnaie. /sɛ bɔ̃ garde la mɔnɛ / – It's ok. Keep the change.

Menu

la portion /la pɔʀsjɔ̃/ – portion

> **demi portion** /demi pɔʀsjɔ̃/ – half portion

> **portion enfant** /pɔʀsjɔ̃ ãfã/ – child portion

le petit–déjeuner /lə p□ti de□œne/ – breakfast

le déjeuner /lə de□œne/ – lunch

le dîner /lə dine/ – dinner

le hors d'oeuvre /lə □□dœv□/ – starter

le plat principal /lə pla pʀɛ̃sipal/ – main course

le repas froid /le repa frwa/ – cold dish

le plats chaud /lə pla ʃo/ – warm dish

la grillade /la gʀijad/ – grilled meat

le repas sans viande /lə repa sã vjãd/ – meal without meat

le dessert /lə desɛʀ/ – dessert

la boisson /la bwasɔ̃/ – drink

Breakfast

le beurre /lə bœ□/ – butter

la confiture /la kɔ̃fityʀ/ – jam

le miel /lə mjɛl/ – honey

les oeufs (m.) /le œ/ – eggs

    sur le plat /syr lə pla/ – fried eggs

    l'omelette /lɔmlɛt/ – omelet

    les oeufs brouillés /le œ b□uje/ – scrambled eggs

    à la coque /le œ a la kɔk/ – boiled eggs

le jambon /lə ʒãbɔ̃/ – ham

    fumé /fyme/ – smoked

    cuit /kɥi/ – cooked

la saucisses /le sosis/ – sausage

le pain

    blanc /bla/ – white

    bis /biz/ – brown

    de seigle /də sɛgl/ – rye

    au lait /o le/ – with milk

le baguette /lə bagɛt/ – baguette

le croissant /lə kʀwasã/ – croissant

Lunch/Diner

Starter

la salade / la salad / – lettuce, salad

la salade de fruits / la salad də fʀɥi / – fruit salad

la pâte de foie / la pat də fwa / – liver paste

la soupe / la sup / – soupe

    de volaille / də vɔlaj / – chicken

de poisson / də *pwasɔ̃* / – fish

bouillon / bujɔ̃ / – broth

le potage / lə *pɔtaʒ* / – pottage

Meat

le boeuf / lə *bœf* / – beef

le canard / lə *kanar* / – duck

le veau / lə *vo* / – veal

le porc / lə *pɔʀ* / – pork

l'agneau (m.) / *laɲo* / – lamb

le lapin / lə *lapɛ̃*/ – rabbit

le sanglier / lə *sɑ̃glije* / – boar

l'oie (f.) / *lwa* / – goose

la dinde / lə *dɛ̃d* / – turkey

le poulet / lə *pulɛ* / – chicken

Fish

l'huitre / *lɥitʀ* / – oyster

le homard / *lɔmaʀ* / – lobster

les moules / *le mul* / – mussel

la truite / *la tʀɥit* / – trout

le silure / lə *silyʀ* / – catfish

Preparation

l'escalope (f.) / *lɛskalɔp* / – escalope, cutlet

de canard / *de canard* / – duck

rôti / *roti* / – roasted meat

de porc / *də pɔʀ* / –pig

d'agneau / *daɲo* / – lamb

de veau / *d vo* / – veal

grillé / *grije* / – grilled

bouilli, cuit / *buji* / / *kɥi* / – cooked

frit / fri / – fried

cru / *kry* / – raw

à la broche / *a la bʀɔʃ* / – on the spit

Spices

le poivre / *lə pwavʀ* / – pepper

le sel / *lə sɛl* / – salt

la cannelle / *la* kanɛl / – cinnamon

l'ail / laj / – garlic

l'oignon / *lɔɲɔ̃* / – onion

le piment / *lə pimã* / – red chilli

Vegetables

les légumes (m.) / *le legym* / – vegetables

le broccoli / *lə bʀɔkɔli* / – broccoli

le célery / *lə sɛləri* / – celery

les champignons (m.) / *le* □ampiŋ□□ / – mushroom

le chou–fleur / l□ □u *flœ*□ / – cauliflower

le chou / *lə ʃu* / – cabbage

le chou de Bruxelles / *lə ʃu d* bʀysɛl / – Brussels sprout

les haricots / *lezariko* / – beans

le petits pois / *lə pti pwa* / – pea

le concombre / *lə kɔ̃kɔ̃bʀ* / – cucumber

le persil / *lə pɛʀsi* / – parsley

le radis / *lə radi* / – radish

l'asperge / *laspɛʀʒ* / – asparagus

la courgette / *la kuʀʒɛt* / – zucchini

la laitue / *la lety* / – lettuce

la lentille / *la lɑ̃tij* / – lens

les haricots verts / *lezariko vɛʀ* / – green beans

la carotte / *la kaʀɔt* / – carrot

le piment / *lə pimɑ̃* / – red chilli

le poireau / *le pwaʀo* / – leek

le poivron / *lə pwavʀɔ̃* / – pepper

la tomate / *la tɔmat* / – tomato

l'épinard / *lepinaʀ* / – spinach

l'asperge / *laspɛʀʒ* / – asparagus

les pommes de terre / *le pɔm d tɛʀ* / – potatoes

l'artichaut / *laʀtiʃo* / – artichoke

Fruits

l'ananas (m.) / *lanana* / – ananas

l'avocat (m.) / *lavɔka* / – avocado

la banana / *la banan* / – banana

la pamplemousse / *la pɑ̃pləmus* / – grapefruit

le kiwi / *lə kivi* / – kiwi

le noix de coco / *lə nwa d koko* / – coconut

la mandarine / la mɑ̃daʁin / – mandarine

la mangue / *la mɑ̃g* / – mango

la grenade / *la gʁənad* / – pomegranate

le raisin / *lə ʁɛzɛ̃* / – grape

      sec / sɛk / – dry grape

la pêche / *la peʃ* / – peach

le melon / *lə melon* / – melon

le raisin / *lə ʁɛzɛ̃* / – grape

la pomme / *la pɔm* / – apple

la fraise / *la fʁɛz* / – strawberry

l'abricot / *labʁiko* / – apricot

la poire / *la pwaʁ* / – pear

la mûre sauvage / *la myʁ sovaʒ* / – wild blackberry

le citron / *lə sitʁɔ̃* / – lemon

la pastèque / *la pastɛk* / – watermelon

la framboise / *la fʁɑ̃bwaz* / – raspberry

l'orange (f.) / *lɔʁɑ̃ʒ* / – orange

la groseille / *la gʁozɛj* / – redcurrant

la figue / *la fig* / – fig

la prune / *la pʁyn* / – plum

la cerise / *la səʁiz* / – cherry

Nuts

l'amande (f.) / *lamãd* / – almond

la noisette / *la nwazɛt* / – hazelnut

la noix / *la nwa* / – walnut

    du Brésil / *dy brezil* / – Brazilian nut

    de cajou / *də kaju* / – cashew nuts

la cacahuète / *la kakaɥɛt* / – peanut

Dessert

le gâteau / *lə gato* / – cake

la tarte / *la tart* / – pie

    aux fraises / *o fʁɛz* / – strawberry pie

    aux noix / *o nwa* / – walnut pie

    aux pommes / *o pom* / – *apple pie*

la crêpe / *la kʁepe* / – pancake

le soufflé au riz / *le sufl o ri* / –rice souffle

la gelée de citron / *la ʒəle d sitʁɔ̃* / – lemon jelly

la glace / *la glas* / – ice cream

    au citron / *o sitʁɔ̃* / – lemon

    à la vanille / *a la vanij* / – vanila

    au chocolat / *o ʃɔkɔla* / – chocolat

aux noisettes / *o nwazɛt* / – hazelnut

Drinks

Non–Alcoholic Drinks

le café / *lə kafe* / – coffee

> **au lait** / *o lɛ* / – with milk

> **noir** / *nwar* / – black coffee

> **turc** / *turk* / – turkish coffee

> **glacé** / *glase* / – ice coffee

> **avec de la crème** / *avek də la krem* / – with cream

le cacao / *lə kakao* / – cocoa

le chocolat / *lə ʃɔkɔla* / – chocolate

le thé / *lə te* / – tea

> **au citron** / *o sitʀɔ̃* / – with lemon

Alcoholic Drinks

l'alcool / *lalkɔl* /– alcohol

le vin / *lə vɛ̃* / – wine

> **de table** / *də tabl* / – table wine

> **vieux** / *vjø* / – old

> **doux** / *du* / – sweet

> **sec** / *sek* / – dry

> **léger** / *leʒe* / – light

> **fort** / *for* / – strong

> **blanc** / *blan* / – white

> **rouge** / *ʀuʒ* /– red

> **de dessert** / *də desɛʀ* / – desert

mousseux / *musø* / – sparkling

le champagne / *lə ʃɑ̃paɲ* /– champagne

le vin en bouteille / *lə vɛ̃ ɑ̃ butɛj* / – wine in a bottle

le cidre / *lə sidʀ* / – cider

le vermouth / *lə vermut* / – vermouth

la bière / *la bjɛʀ* / – beer

    ambre / *ambre* /– amber

    à la pression / *a la pʀesjɔ̃* / – draft beer

    blonde / *blond* / – blonde

    brune / *bryn* / – dark beer

    sans alcool / *sɑ̃zalkol* / – without alcohol

l'eau de vie / *lo d vi* / – brandy

Whisky / *lə viski* / – whisky

le cognac / *lə kɔɲak* / – cognac

le rhum / *lə ʀɔm* / – rum

la liqueur / *la likœ□* / – liqueur

Chapter 13: Shopping

L'élégance est une question de personnalité, plus que de vêtements.

Jean Paul Sartre

It's hard to imagine a day without shopping. If you're traveling or living in France, you'll need this chapter almost every day. There are two words associated with shopping: "*vendre* (to sell) and "*acheter*" (to purchase).

vendre / *vãdʀ* / – to sell

acheter / *aʃəte* / – to buy

le magasin / *lə magazɛ̃* / – store

la boutique / *la butik* / – shop, boutique

le marchand / *lə maʀʃã* / – shopkeeper

la vendeuse / *la v□□dœz* / – shop assistant, female

le vendeur / *lə v□□dœ□* / – shop assistant, male

l'échantillon / *leʃãtijɔ̃* / – sample

le client / *l klijã* / – client

les soldes / *le sɔld* / – sale

payer en espèces / *peje ã ɛspɛsə* / – to pay with cash

par carte / *paʀ kart* / – with credit card

la cabine d'essayage / *la kabin desɛjaʒ* / – fitting room

le prix / *lə pri* / – price

fixe / *fiks* / – fixed

reduit / *ʀedɥi* / – reduced

la note / *la not* / – bill

Basic Phrases

Upon entering a local shop, you may hear:

Bonjour Monsieur/Madame ! Que désirez-vous ? / *bɔ̃ʒuʀ məsjø/madam / kə dezire vu /*– Good day Mr/Madam! What would you like?

> **Je désire / J'ai besoin ( ).** / *ʒə deziʀ / ʒe bəzwɛ̃ /* – I would like / I need ().

> **Avez-vous ( ) ?** / *ave vu ( ) /* – Do you have ( )?

Je voudrais aller faire les magasins. / *ʒə vudʀɛ ale fɛʀ le magazɛ̃ /* – I would like to go shopping.

Où est-ce que je peux acheter/trouver ( ) ? / *u esk ʒə pø aʃəte / truve /* – Where can I buy/find ( )?

Où est l'hypermarché le plus proche ? / *u e lipɛʀmaʀʃe lə ply pʀɔʃ /*– Where is the nearest hypermarket?

Vous avez ( ) ? /*vuzave …/*– Do you have ( )?

Je peux voir ( ) ? / *ʒə pø vwar /* –Can I see ( )?

Y a–t–il des soldes ? / *jatil de sold /* – Are there sales?

C'est soldé aussi ? / *sɛ solde osi /* – Is it on sale too?

Veuillez me montrer ( ). / *vøje mə montre () /* – Please show me ( ).

Vous me recommandez lequel ? / *vu m ʀəkɔmɑ̃de lə kɛl /* – Which one do you recommend me?

Je le/la/les prends. / *ʒə lə/la/le pʀɑ̃d /* – I'll take it.

Il y avait un prix réduit sur l'étiquette ? / *iljave œ□ pri □ed□i syr letik□t* / – Was there a reduced price on the label?

Je peux avoir un sac ? / *ʒə pø avwar œ□ sak* / – Can I have a bag?

Vous pouvez l'emballer ? / *vu puve mãbale* / – Can you wrap it?

Warranty

Vous offrez une garantie de remboursement ? / *vuzofʀe yn gaʀãti də ʀãbuʀsəmã* / – Do you offer a money back guarantee?

Quelle est la durée de la garantie ? / *kɛl e la dyre de la gaʀãti* / – How long is the warranty?

Est-ce que la garantie couvre aussi ( ) ? / *ɛsk la gaʀãti kuvʀ osi* / – Does the waranty also cover ( )?

Comment faire pour obtenir la garantie ? / *kɔmã fɛʀ puʀ ɔptəniʀ la gaʀãti* / – How do I get the warranty?

Reclamation

Je veux faire une réclamation sur ce produit. / *ʒə vø fɛʀ yn ʀeklamasjɔ̃ syr s pʀɔdɥi* / – I want to make a reclamation for this product.

Ça ne marche plus. / *sa n maʀʃ ply* / – It does not work anymore.

J'ai suivi le mode d'emploi. / *ʒɛ suivi lə mod dãplwa* / – I followed the manual.

Voici le ticket de caisse. / *vwasi lə tike də kɛs* / – Here is the receipt.

Vous pouvez me l'échanger ? / *vu puve mə leʃãʒe* / – Can you exchange it for me?

Je veux être remboursé. / *ʒə vø ɛtr ʀãbuʀse* / – I would like to be reimbursed.

137

Pouvez-vous me prévenir par mail ? / *vu puve mə prevənir par mɛl* / – Could you notify me by email?

Votre réclamation a été rejetée ? / *votr reklamasjɔ̃ a ete rəʒəte* / – Has your claim been rejected?

Pourquoi ma réclamation a été rejetée ? / *purkwa ma reklamasjɔ̃ a ete rəʒəte* / – Why was my claim rejected?

Paying

Ca coûte combien ? / *sa kut kɔ̃bjɛ̃* / – How much is it?

C'est trop cher. / *sɛ tro ʃɛr* / – It's too expensive.

Ce n'est pas cher. / *sə nɛ pa ʃɛr* /– It is cheap.

Je n'ai pas assez d'argent. / *ʒə nɛ pa ase darʒã* / – I do not have enough money.

Je paye où ? / *ʒə pɛj u*/ Where do I pay?

Où est la caisse ? / *u ɛ la kɛs* / – Where is the check out?

Je peux payer en liquide ? / *ʒə pø pɛje ã likid* / – Could I pay in cash?

Je n'ai pas de monnaie. / *ʒə nɛ pa də mɔnɛ* / – I don't have change.

Vous acceptez ces chèques ? / *vuzaksɛpte se ʃɛk* / – Do you accept these checks?

Je vais payer par carte. / *ʒə vɛ pɛje par kart* / – I'll pay by card.

Je ne trouve pas mon portefeuille. / □□ n□ pø pa truve m□□ p□□t□fœj /– I can't find my wallet.

Vous pouvez me prêter quelques euros ? / *vu puve mə prete kɛlkzøro* / – Can you lend me a few euros?

Comment je fais pour obtenir le remboursement de la T.V.A ? / kɔmã ʒə fɛ pur ɔptənir lə rãbursəmã də la tva / — How do I get VAT refund?

Shops

la bouquinerie / la bukineri / – bookstore

la librairie / la libreri / – library

la pharmacie / la farmasi / – pharmacy

la boucherie / la buʃri / – butcher

la parfumerie / la parfymri / – perfumery

la boulangerie / la bulãʒri / – bakery

la poissonnerie / la pwasɔnri / – fish shop

le grand–magasin / lə grã magazẽ/ – department store

la pêtisserie / la patisri / – cake shop, confectionery

le bureau de tabac / lə byro də taba / – tobacco store

Supermarket

Ingredients

la farine / la farin /– flour

le pain / lə pẽ / – bread

l'oeuf (m.) / lœf / – egg

le yaourt / lə jaurt / – yoghurt

le lait fermentée / lə lɛ fɛrmãte / fermented milk

les petits pains / le pti pẽ / – buns

la levure / la levyr /– yeast

le miel / *lə mjɛl* / – honey

le fromage / *lə fʀɔmaʒ* / – cheese

le lait / *lə lɛ* / – milk

le muesli / *lə myysli* / – muesli

la pâte à tartiner / *la pat a tartine* / – spread

le beurre / *lə bœ□* / – butter

le moutarde / *lə mutaʀd* / – mustard

le saucisson / *lə sosisɔ̃* / – salami

le vinaigre / *lə vinɛgʀ* / – vinegar

le bacon / *le bekɔn* / – bacon

le sucre / *lə sykʀ* / – sugar

le sel / *lə sɛl* / – salt

le jambon / *lə ʒɑ̃bɔ̃* / – ham

le fromage / *lə fʀɔmaʒ* / – cheese

- **emmental** / *emɛ̃tal* / – emmental
- **de brebis** / *də bʀəbi* / – sheep
- **en tranches** / *ɑ̃ tʀɑ̃ʃ* / – in slices
- **bleu** / *blø* / – blue
- **fondu** / *fɔ̃dy* / – melted

Clothes

les vêtements (m.) / *le vɛtmɑ̃* / – clothes

le tee-shirt / *lə ti□œ□t* / – T-shirt

    à manches courtes / *a mɑ̃ʃ kur* / – short sleeves

    à manches longues / *a mɑ̃ʃ long* / – long sleeves

polo / polo / – polo

la chemise / *la ʃəmiz* / – shirt

le sweat–shirt / *lə swit☐œ☐t* / – sweatshirt

le pull / *lə pyl* / – sweater

le blouson / *lə bluzɔ̃* / – jacket

L'anorak (m.) / *lanɔʀak* / – anorak

le manteau / *lə mɑ̃to* / – coat

le costume / *lə kɔstym* / – suit

la veste / *la vɛst* / – jacket

le gilet / *lə ʒilɛ* / – waistcoat

la robe / *la rob* /– dress

le pantalon / *lə pɑ̃talɔ̃* / – pantalon

le jean / *lə dʒin* / – jeans

le short / *lə ʃɔʀt* / – shorts

la jupe / *la ʒyp* / – skirt

le pyjama / *lə piʒama* / – pajama

le sous–vêtement/ *lə suvɛtmɑ̃* / – underwear

- **la culotte** / *la kylɔt* / – knickers

- **le soutien–gorge** / *lə sutjɛ̃gɔʀʒ* /– bra

- **le slip** / *lə slip* /– knickers slip

les chaussettes / *lə ʃosɛt* / – socks

l'imperméable (m.) / *lɛ̃pɛʀmeabl* / – raincoat

la jambe / *la ʒɑ̃b* / – trouser leg

la manche / *la mɑ̃ʃ* / – sleeve

le col / *lə kɔl* / – collar

la taille / *la taj* / – size

la longueur / *la l□□□œ□* / – length

à boutons / *a buton* / – with buttons

à fermeture éclair / *a fɛʀmətyʀ eklɛʀ* / – with zipper

Accessoires

la ceinture / *la sɛ̃tyʀ* / – belt

les boutons (m.) / *le butɔ̃* / – buttons

le bracelet / *lə bʀaslɛ* / – bracelet

la chaîne / *la ʃɛn* / – chain

la boucle d'oreille / *lə bukl dɔʀɛj* / – earring

le sac à main / *lə sak a mɛ̃* / – handbag

le parapluie / *lə paʀaplɥi* / – rain

le bonnet / *lə bɔnɛ* / – a wolly hat

le chapeau / *lə ʃapo* / – hat

l'écharpe (f.) / *leʃaʀp* / – scarf

le foulard / *lə fulaʀ* / – a silk scarf

les gants (m.) / *le gɑ̃* / – gloves

les lunettes de soleil / *le lynet d sɔlɛj* / – sunglasses

Shoes

les chaussures sans talons / *le ʃosyʀ sɑ̃ talɔ̃* / – shoes without heels

les chaussures à talons hauts / *le ʃosyʀ a talɔ̃ ho* / – high–heeled shoes

les soulier bas / *le sulje ba* / – flat shoes

les mocassins (m.) / *le mɔkasɛ̃* / – mocassins

les chaussures de sport / *le ʃosyʀ d spoʀ* / – sneakers

les tennis / *le tenis* / – tennis

les chaussures de marche/montagne / *le ʃosyʀ d maʀʃ/ mɔ̃taɲ* / – hiking shoes

les sandales (f.) / *le sɑ̃dal* / – sandals

les bottes (f.) / *les bot* / – boots

les pantoufles (f.) / *le pɑ̃tufl* / – slippers

Common Phrases

J'ai vu en vitrine. / *ʒə vy un vitrin* / – I saw in the window display.

Il me faudrait la taille ( ) . / *il m fodre la taj* / – I would need the size ( ).

Puis-je l'essayer ? / *pɥi ʒə eseje* / – Could I try it on?

C'est trop / *sɛ tro* / – It is too

    grand / *gʀɑ̃* / – big

    petit / *pti* / – small

    large / *laʀʒ* / – wide

    étroit / *etʀwa* / – tight

    foncé / *fɔ̃se* / – dark

    clair / *klɛʀ* / – light

La qualité (couleur) ne me plaît pas. / *la kalite / kulœ☐ / nə mə plɛ pa* / / – I don't like the quality (color).

La couleur est–elle permanente ? / *la kulœ☐ ☐tel p☐rman☐☐t☐* / – Is the color permanent?

Avez-vous quelque chose de moins cher ? / *ave vu kɛlk ʃoz də mwɛ̃ ʃer* / – Do you have something cheaper?

Combien coûte une pièce/paire de ( )? / *kɔ̃bjɛ̃ kut yn pjɛs/pɛrə də (* *) /* – How much does an item/pair of ( ) cost?

Cela ne me va pas. / *səla nə mə va pa /* – It doesn't suit me.

Puis-je échanger cela ? / *pɥi ʒə eʃɑ̃ʒe səla /* – Could I exchange that?

Chapter 14: Bank / Exchange Office / Post Office

Les défis sont ce qui rend la vie intéressante et les surmonter est ce qui donne sens à la vie.

Joshua J. Marine

In France, banks are generally open Monday through Friday from 08:30-17:30, although most of them close between 12 p.m. and 14 p.m. for lunch. In some cases, banks may be open on Saturday mornings but closed on Mondays, so be sure to check before heading out.

le compte bancaire / *lə kɔ̃t bãkɛʀ* / – bank account

    compte courant / *kɔ̃t kuʀã* / – current account

    compte en devises / *kɔ̃t ã dəviz* / – currency account

l'ordre de virement (bancaire) (m.) / *lɔʀdʀ viʀmã* / – bank transfer

la pièce de monnaie / *la pjɛs d mɔnɛ* / – change

le billet de banque / *lə bijɛ d bãk* / – banknote

le guichet / *lə giʃɛ* / – counter

le solde du compte / *lə sɔld dy kɔ̃t* / – account balance

le distributeur de billets / *lə dist☐ibytœ☐ d bijɛ* / – cash machine

Exchanging money / ATM

Je veux changer de l'argent. / ʒə vø ʃɑ̃ʒe də laʀʒɑ̃ / – I would like to exchange money.

Il y a une commission ? / ilja yn kɔmisjɔ̃ / – Is there a commission?

Combien d'argent faut-il changer ? / kɔ̃bjɛ̃ daʀʒɑ̃ fotil ʃɑ̃ʒe / – How much money should I exchange?

Vous pouvez m'échanger un billet de cinquante euros ? / vu puve me□□□□e œ□ bij□ d s□□k□□t ø□o / Could you exchange me a fifty euro banknote?

Je cherche un bureau de change. / □□ □□□□e œ□ by□o d□ □□□□ / I am looking for a currency exchange office.

Je voudrais retirer de l'argent. / ʒə vudʀɛ retire də laʀʒɑ̃ / I would like to withdraw money.

Le distributeur a avalé ma carte. / l□ dist□ibytœ□ a avale ma kart / – The ATM swallowed my card.

Le distributeur refuse ma carte. / l□ dist□ibytœ□ refuz ma kart / – The ATM refuses my card. /

Bank

J'aimerais ouvrir un compte chez vous. / □emre ouvrir œ□ k□□t □e vu / – I would like to open an account here.

Il me faudra quels documents ? / il me fodʀa kɛl dɔkymɑ̃ / – What documents will I need?

Quel est votre numéro de compte ? / kɛl e votr nymeʀo dkɔ̃t / – What is your account number?

Je veux retirer de l'argent de mon compte. / ʒə vø ʀətire de laʀʒɑ̃ də mɔ̃ kɔ̃t / – I would like to withdraw money from my account.

Quel est le montant de retrait minimal/maximal possible ? / *kɛl e lə mɔ̃tã de ʀətʀɛ minimal/maksimal* / – What is the minimum/maximum possible withdrawal amount ?

Quel est le solde de mon compte ? / *kɛl e lə sɔld d mɔ̃ kɔ̃t* / – What is my account balance?

Je voudrais payer par virement bancaire. / *ʒə vudʀɛ peje par viʀmã bãkɛʀ* / – I would like to pay by bank transfer.

Le virement va prendre combien de temps ? / *lə viʀmã va pʀãdʀ kɔ̃bjɛ̃ də tã* / – How long will the transfer take?

Il faut aller à quel guichet ? / *il fo ale a kɛl giʃɛ* / – Which counter should I go to?

Apple Pay

Connecting on Apple Pay

Connectez-vous à l'Apple Store. / *kɔnɛkte vu a lApple Store* / – Log in to the Apple Store.

Créer votre identifiant. / *kree votr idãtifjã* / – Create your ID.

Vous avez déjà un identifiant Apple ? Retrouvez-le ici. / *vuzave de□a œ□ id□□tifj□□ (apple) □□t□uve l□ isi* / – Already have an Apple ID? Find it here.

Saisissez les informations ci-dessous pour retrouver votre identifiant Apple. / *sezise lez ɛ̃fɔʀmasjɔ̃ si desu puʀ retruve votr idãtifjã (apple)* / – Enter the information below to find your Apple ID.

Saisissez les caractères / *sezise le kaʀaktɛʀ* / – Enter the characters.

Mot de passe oublié / *mo d pas ublije* / – Forgoten password.

Valider à l'aide d'un sms / appel téléphonique / *valide a l□d dœ□ esemes / ap□le telef□nik* / – Validate with an sms / phone call.

Cette adresse sera votre nouvel identifiant. / *set adres sera votr nuvel idãtifjã* / – This address will be your new username.

Le nouveau code / *lə nuvo kod* / The new code.

Shopping on Apple Pay

Poursuivre vos achats / *puʀsɥivʀ voz aʃa* / – Continue shopping.

Votre panier est vide / *votr panje e vid* / – Your basket is empty.

Votre sélection / *votr selɛksjɔ̃* / – Your selection.

Commandes / *kɔmãd* / – Orders.

Compte / *kɔ̃* / – Account

Connectez-vous pour régler vos achats plus rapidement. / *kɔnɛkte vu pur regle voz aʃa ply ʀapidmã* / Log in to pay for your purchases faster.

Besoin d'une aide supplémentaire ? / *bəzwɛ̃ dyn ɛd syplemãtɛʀ* / – Do you need additional help?

Post Office

Post offices are marked in blue with the inscription "*la poste*" or "*PTT*". The main post office is open on weekdays from 8–17 pm and on Saturdays till 12 PM. Stamps can be bought at post offices or at tabac stores.

la poste / *la post* / – poste

la lettre / *la letr* / – letter

la carte postale / *la kart postal* / – postcard

le collis / *lə koli* / – paquet

le timbre / *lə tɛ̃bʀ* / – stamp

l'enveloppe (f.) / *lãvəlɔp* / – envelope

la rue / *la ry/* – street

la ville / *la vil* / – city

le code postal / *lə kod postal* / postal code

en recommandée / *ã ʀəkɔmãde* / registered

par avion / *par avjɔ̃* / – by airplane

express / *ɛkspʀɛ* / express

J'aimerais envoyer une lettre recommandée. / *ʒəmre ãvwaje yn letr ʀəkɔmãde* / – I would like to send a registered letter.

Tarif lent, s'il vous plaît. / *tarif lã sil vu plɛ* / – Regular fare, please.

Une enveloppe / un timbre s'il vous plaît. /*yn ãvəlɔp/* œ□ *t□□b□* / sil vu plɛ / – An enveloppe / a stamp please.

Il me faut quel timbre pour ( ) ? / *il m fo kɛl tɛ̃bʀ pur* / – What stamp do I need for ( )?

Combien coûte d'envoyer un colis de 1 kilo ? / *k□□bjɔ̃□ kut d□□vwaje un koli d œ□ kilo* / – What is the cost of sending a package weighing 1 kilo?

C'est quel guichet pour envoyer une lettre ? / *sɛ kɛl giʃɛ pur ãvwaje yn lɛtʀ* / – Which counter is it to send a letter?

Chapter 15: Business

La seule limite à notre épanouissement de demain sera nos doutes d'aujourd'hui.

Franklin D. Roosevelt

Learning some basic French phrases is highly recommended if you intend to settle business in France or if you are looking to work there. They will praise you if you are struggling and return to English. The value of patience will be appreciated in business communication, whereas the value of pressure will be negatively viewed. The same goes for aggressive selling techniques, it won't generate a positive response. You should instead focus on discussion and information exchange. Also, avoid discussing personal matters during business negotiations.

L'emploi (m.) / *lãplwa* / – employment

le travail / le boulot / *lə tʀavaj* / *lə bulo* / – job

> **le petit boulot d'étudiant** / *lə pəti bulo detydjã* / – student job

> **le travail d'été** / *lə travaj dete* / – summer job

le travailleur temporaire / *lə t☐avajœ☐ t☐☐p☐☐☐☐* / – temporary worker

le stage / *lə staʒ* / – internship

embaucher, employer / *ãboʃe/ ãplwaje* / – to hire

le contrat de travail / *lə kɔ̃tʀa d tʀavaj* / – employment contract

le contrat à durée / *lə kɔ̃tʀa a dyre* / – term contract

determinée (CDD) / *determine* / – definite time

indeterminée (CDI) / *ɛ̃detɛʀmine* / – indefinite time

le congé / *lə kɔ̃ʒe* / – annual leave

la démission / *la demisjɔ̃* / – resignation

le délais de préavis / *lə delɛ d pʀeavi* / – notice period

le salaire / *lə salɛʀ* / – the salary

le salaire horaire / *lə salɛʀ ɔʀɛʀ* / – the hourly wage

le salaire mensuel / *lə salɛʀ mɑ̃sɥɛl* / – the monthly salary

le revenu brut / *lə ʀ(ə)v(ə)ny bʀyt* / – the gross income

le revenu net / *lə ʀ(ə)v(ə)ny nɛt* / – the net income

le chèque de paie / *lə ʃɛk d pɛ* / – the paycheck

l'augmentation du salaire / *lɔgmɑ̃tasjɔ̃ dy salɛʀ* / – the salary increase

L'équipe (f.) / *lekip* / – team

    l'équipe du matin / *lekip dy matɛ̃* / – morning team

    l'équipe de l'après-midi / *lekip de lapʀɛ midi* / – afternoon team

    l'équipe de nuit / *lekip de nɥi* / – night team

les heures supplémentaires / *lezœ□ syplem□□t□□* / – overtime work

    rémunération des heures supplémentaires / *ʀemyneʀasjɔ̃ dezœ□ syplem□□t□□* / – overtime work payment

la prestation maladie / *la pʀɛstasjɔ̃ maladi* / – sickness benefit

les avantages annexes/sociaux / *lezavɑ̃taʒ anɛks / sɔsjal* / – additional benefits

le congé / les vacances / lə kɔ̃ʒe / le vakans / – vacation

le tickets/chèques restaurant / lə tikɛ / lə ʃɛk ʀɛstɔʀɑ̃ / – restaurant vouchers

la voiture de fonction / la vwatyʀ d fɔ̃ksjɔ̃ / – company car

le travail à plein temps / lə tʀavaj a plɛ̃ tɑ̃ / – a full-time job

le travail à temps partiel / lə mi–temps a tɑ̃ paʀsjɛl / – part-time work

la journée de travail / la ʒuʀne d tʀavaj / – working day

durée/temps/heures de travail / dyre / t□□ / œ□ də tʀavaj / – duration/time/hours of work.

About my Job

Où travaillez-vous? / u tʀavaje vu /– Where do you work?

Quelle est votre profession ? / kɛl e votr pʀɔfesjɔ̃ / – What is your profession?

> **Je suis ( ).** / ʒə sɥi / – I am ( ).

> **Je travaille comme ( ).** / ʒə tʀavaje kom / – I work as ( ).

Depuis combien de temps vous travaillez là-bas ? / dəpɥi kɔ̃bjɛ̃ d tɑ̃ vu tʀavaje la ba / – How long have you been working there?

> **Ça fait plus de cinq ans que je travaille ici.** / sa fɛ ply d sɛ̃k ɑ̃ ʒə tʀavaj isi / – I have worked here for more than five years.

Je travaille à temps partiel/plein temps. / ʒə travaj a tɑ̃ parsjel/plɛ̃ tɑ̃ / – I work part–time/ full–time.

Je fais des heures supplémentaires. / □□ f□ dezœ□ syplem□□t□□ / – I work overtime.

J'ai deux emplois. / ʒɛ dø ɑ̃plwa / – I have two jobs.

Je suis au chômage. / *ʒə sчi o ʃomaʒ* / – I am unemployed.

J'ai pris ma retraite. / *ʒɛ pri ma ʀətʀɛt* / – I am retired.

At work

À quelle heure tu commences à travailler ? / *a k□l œ□ ty k□m□□se a travaje* / – What time do you start working?

> **Je travaille de neuf à six heures.** / *ʒə travaj də nœf a siz œ□* / – I work from nine to six.

J'ai un horaire flexible. / *ʒɛ œ□ □□□□ fl□ksibl* / – I have a flexible schedule.

Vous travaillez par relais ? / *vu travaje par ʀəlɛ* / – Do you work in shifts?

Est-ce que les heures supplémentaires de travail sont payées ? / *ɛsk lezœ□ syplem□□t□□ d travaj son pɛje* / – Is working extra hours payed ?

J'ai droit à combien de jours de congé ? / *ʒɛ drwa a kɔ̃bjɛ̃ də ʒuʀ də kɔ̃ʒe* / – How many days off am I entitled to ?

Je vais prendre un congé lundi prochain. / *ʒɛ vɛ pʀɑ̃dʀ œ□ k□□□e lœ□di p□□□□□* / – I am going to take a day off next Monday.

Est-ce que je peux prendre un congé non payé ? / *ɛsk ʒə pø p□□□d□ œ□ k□□□e n□□ peje* / – Can I take unpaid leave ?

Je vais en voyage d'affaires en Allemagne. / *ʒə vɛ □□ vwaja□ daf□□ œ□ alma□* / – I am going on a business trip to Germany.

Il faut que je parte plus tôt aujourd'hui. / *il fɛ k ʒə part ply to oʒuʀdчi* / – I have to leave earlier today.

Je suis en congé maladie. / *ʒə sчi ɑ̃ kɔ̃ʒe maladi* / – I am on sick leave.

Applying for a Job

l'agence nationale pour l'emploi / *laʒɑ̃s nasjɔnal pur lɑ̃plwa* / – national employment agency

l'agence/bureau de placement / *laʒɑ̃s/byro d plasmɑ̃* / – placement agency/office

l'offre d'emploi / *lɔfʀ dɑ̃plwa* / – job offer

les petites annonces / *le ptit anɔ̃s* / – ads

l'entretien d'embauche / *ɑ̃tʀətjɛ̃ dɑ̃boʃ* / – job interview

CV / *seve* / – resume

Je cherche un boulot pour les vacances. / □□ □□□□e œ□ *bulo pur le vakɑ̃s* / – I am looking for a job for the holidays.

Je cherche un boulot d'étudiant. / □□ □□□□e œ□ *bulo detydj□□* / – I am looking for a student job.

Je veux trouver un petit boulot à l'étranger. / □□ *vø truve* œ□ *pti bulo al et□□□□e* / – I want to find a little job abroad.

Je voudrais travailler / *ʒə vudʀɛ travaje* / – I would like to work

    à mi–temps / *a mi tɑ̃* / – part–time

    à plein temps / *a plɛ̃ tɑ̃* / – full time

En quoi consisterait le travail exactement ? / *ɑ̃ kwa kɔ̃siste l̩ tʀavaj ɛgzaktəmɑ̃* / What would the job entail?

Quand je pourrais commencer à travailler? / *kɑ̃ ʒə puʀɛ kɔmɑ̃se a travaje* / – When can I start working?

Est-ce que quelqu'un pourrait me montrer quoi faire ? / □sk *k□lkœ□ puʀ□ m□ m□□t□e kwa f□r* / – Could someone show me what to do?

Chapter 16: Health and Wellbeing

J'ai décidé d'être heureux parce que c'est bon pour la santé.

Voltaire

It happens often in France that you can't recognize the doctor from a nurse, as they rarely wear the traditional white doctor robes you're used to seeing in your country. Usually, the doctor will greet you in the waiting room instead of having a nurse calling your name while you wait. There is no need for you to arrive early most of the time, and you are perfectly fine if you are a few minutes late. When you enter a waiting room, don't ignore the other people. It's considered rude to simply sit down without saying a *bonjour*.

Body

les reins (m.) /*le ʀɛ̃*/ – kidneys

l'intestin (m.) /*lɛ̃tɛstɛ̃*/ – the intestine

la tête /*la tɛt*/ – the head

la gorge /*la gɔʀʒ*/ – the throat

le sein /*lə sɛ̃*/ – the breast

le foie /*lə fwa*/ – liver

la langue /*la lɑ̃g*/ – tongue

le dos /*lə do*/ – the back

les cheveux /le ʃevo/ – hair

l'os (m.) /lɔs/ – bone

la peau /la po/ – the skin

le sang /lə sɑ̃/ – the blood

le muscle /lə myskl/ – the muscle

le cerveau /lə sɛʁvo/ – the brain

la jambe / la ʒɑ̃b / – the leg

le nez / lə ne / – the nose

le poumon / lə pumɔ̃ / – the lung

la poitrine / la pwatʁin / – the chest

le doigt / lə dwa / – the finger

le bras / lə bra / – the arm

les organes génitaux / lezorgan ʒenito / – genitals

le coeur / lə kœ□ / – the heart

le cou / lə ku / – the neck

la dent / la dɑ̃ / – the tooth

l'estomac (m.) / lɛstɔma / – stomach

la veine / la vɛn / – vein

le nerf / lə nɛʁ / – nerve

la glande / la glɑ̃d / – glande

la bile / la bil / – bile

At the Doctor

To make an appointment with a doctor in France, you call the *"cabinet medical"* and you say *"je voudrais prendre rendez-vous s'il vous plaît"* – "I'd like to make an appointment please" and a secretary will arrange the appointment.

le medécin / *lə medəsɛ̃* / – doctor

le spécialiste / *lə spesjalist* / – specialist

l'infirmière / *lɛ̃fiʀmje* / – the nurse

la maladie / *la maladi* / – the disease

> **bénigne** / *benɛ̃* / – mild

> **grave** / *grav* / – severe

la feuille de maladie / *la fœj d maladi* / sickness sheet

la plaie / *la plɛ* / – the wound

le régime alimentaire / *lə reʒim alimãtɛrə* / – the diet

la grossesse / *la groses* / – the pregnancy

l'accouchement (m.)/ *lakuʃmã* / – childbirth

On a besoin d'un médecin. / ☐☐ a b☐zw☐☐ dœ☐ med(☐)s☐☐ / – We need a doctor.

Envoyer une ambulance à ( ) / *ãvwaje yn ãbylãs* / – Send ambulance to ( ).

Quelles sont les heures de consultation ? / k☐l s☐☐ lezœ☐ dk☐☐syltasj☐☐ / – What are the consultation hours?

The doctor may ask you questions like these:

- **De quoi vous plaignez-vous ?** / *də kwa pleɲe vu* / – What are you complaining about?

- **Où avez-vous mal ?** / *u ave vu mal* / – Where does it hurt?

   J'ai mal / *ʒɛ mal* / – I have pain

   - **à la tête** / *a la tɛt* / – in head
   - **à la gorge** / *a la gɔʀʒ* / – in throat
   - **à l'estomac** / *a lɛstɔma* / – in stomac
   - **à l'oreille** / *a lɔʀɛj* / – in ear

   J'ai de la fièvre. / *ʒɛ də la fjɛvʀ* / – I have a fever.

   Je souffre d'insomnie. / *ʒə sufr dɛ̃sɔmni* / I suffer from insomnia.

   Je me suis évanoui. / *ʒə m sɥi evanoui* / – I fainted.

   Je tousse beaucoup. / *ʒə tus boku* / – I cough a lot.

   Je suis très fatigué. / *ʒə sɥi tre fatige* / – I am very tired.

   J'ai du mal à respirer. / – *ʒɛ dy mal a respirer* / – I have trouble breathing.

   J'ai pris froid. / *ʒɛ pri frwa* / – I caught a cold.

   J'ai froid/chaud. / *ʒɛ frwa/ ʃo* / I am cold/hot.

   J'ai des vomissements. / *ʒɛ de vɔmismã* / – I vomit.

   J'ai de la constipation. / *ʒɛ d la kɔ̃stipasjɔ̃* / I have constipation.

   J'ai des palpitations. / *ʒɛ de palpitasjɔ̃* / I have palpitations.

   Je suis allergique à /*ʒə sɥi alɛʀʒik a*/ – I am allergic to...

   J'ai une éruption de boutons. / *ʒɛ yn eʀypsjɔ̃ d buton* / – I have a rash.

Ça démange terriblement. / *sa demãʒe тeʀibləmã* / – It itches terribly.

Je me suis fait piquer par un insecte. / □□ *m*□ *s*□*i f*□ *pike par œ*□ □□*s*□*kt* / I got stung by an insect.

La tête me tourne. / *la tet mə тuʀn* / – I feel dizzy.

J'ai un problème avec / □□ *œ*□ *p*□□*bl*□*m av*□*k* / – I have a problem with

> **la jambe** / *la ʒãb* / – leg

> **le bras** / *lə bra* / – arm

Je ne peux pas bouger le bras. / *ʒə n pø pq buʒe lə bra* / – I can't move my arm.

Je me sens trés mal. / *ʒə m sã тʀɛ mal* / – I feel very bad.

- **Depuis quand souffrez–vous ?** / *dəpɥi kã sufre vu* / – How long have you been in pain?

> **Depuis hier soir.** / *dəpɥi jɛʀ swar* / – Since yesterday evening.

> **Ça dure trois jours.** / *sa dyr trwa ʒuʀ* / – It has been three days.

- **Est-ce que vous digérez bien?** / *esk vu diʒeʀe bjẽ* / – Are you digesting well?

> **Je digère mal.** / *ʒə diʒɛʀ mal* / – I digest badly.

- **Avez-vous de l'appétit ?** / *ave vu d lapeti* / – Do you have appetite?

> **Je n'ai goût à rien.** / *ʒə nɛ gu a ʀjẽ* / – I don't have the sense of taste.

- **Allez-vous à la selle regulièrement ?** / *ave vu a sel ʀegyljɛʀmã* / – Do you go to the bathroom regularly?

- **Est-ce que je vous fais mal ici ?** / *esk ʒə vu fɛ mal isi* / – Does it hurt when I press here?

The doctor may also ask you to do something-

- **Déshabillez-vous jusqu'à la ceinture.** / *dezabije vu ʒyska la sɛ̃tyʀ* / – Undress to the waist.

- **Faites voir votre langue.** / *fɛt vwar votr lãg* / – Show me your tongue.

- **Ouvrez la bouche.** / *uvʀe la buʃ* / – Open your mouth.

- **Inspirez profondément !** / *ɛ̃spiʀe pʀɔfɔ̃demã* / – Take a deep breath !

>   **par la bouche** / *par la buʃ* / – through the mouth

>   **par le nez** / *par lə ne* / – through the nose

- **Ne respirez pas !** / *nə ʀɛspiʀe pa* / – Don't breathe !

You may additionally ask questions like these:

>   **C'est contagieux ?** / *sɛ kɔ̃taʒjø* / – Is it contagious?

>   **C'est grave ?** / *sɛ grav* / – Is it serious?

>   **Je dois prendre le médicament pendant combien de temps ?** / *ʒə dwa pʀɑ̃dʀ lə medikamã pãdã kɔ̃bjɛ̃ də tã* / – For how long should I take the medicine?

>   **Quels examens il me faudra passer ?** / *kɛl ɛgzamɛ̃ il m fodʀa pase* / – What examinations will I need to pass?

>   **J'ai besoin de mon médicament.** / *ʒɛ bəzwɛ̃ də mon medikamã* / – I need my medicine.

J'ai une assurance maladie. / *ʒɛ yn asyʀãs maladi* / – I have a health insurance.

At the Dentist

J'ai / ʒɛ / – I have

    mal de dents / mal də dã / – toothache

    les dents sensibles / le dã sãsibl / – sensitive teeth

    les gencives douloureuses / le ʒãsiv duluʀøz / – sore gums

    mauvaise haleine / mɔvɛz alɛn / – bad breath

    une carie / yn kari / – caries

    une gingivite / yn ʒɛ̃ʒivit / – a gingivitis

    de la plaque / də la plak / –plaque

    une dent cassée / yn dã kase / – a broken teeth

    une infection / lɛ̃fɛksjɔ̃ / – an infection

Puis-je prendre rendez-vous chez le dentiste ? / pɥi ʒə pʀãdʀ ʀãdevu ʃe lə dãtist / – Can I book an appointment at the dentist?

Je dois décaler mon rendez-vous chez le dentiste. / ʒə dwa dekale mɔ̃ ʀãdevu ʃe lə dãtist / – I have to reschedule my dentist appointment.

Un de mes plombages est parti. / œ□ d□ me pl□□ba□ e parti / – One of my fillings is gone.

J'ai eu des douleurs aux gencives récemment. / □□ y de dulœ□ o □□□siv □esam□□ / – I have had gum pain recently.

S'il vous plaît, inclinez-vous et ouvrez la bouche. / sil vu plɛ ɛ̃kline vu e uvre la buʃ / – Please, bow down and open your mouth.

Tenez, enfilez ce tablier de protection. / tene ãfile s tablije də pʀɔtɛksjɔ̃ / – Here, put on this protective apron.

Vous avez une inflammation des gencives. / vuzave yn ɛ̃flamasjɔ̃ de ʒãsiv / – You have some inflammation of the gums.

Il faut faire une nouvelle série de radiographies. / *il fo fɛr yn nuvel seri də radiografi* / – A new series of x–rays should be done.

Il semble que vous ayez quelques caries. / *il sembl k vuzave kɛlk kari* / – It looks like you have caries.

At the Pharmacy

le sparadrap / *lə sparadra* / – the medical plaster

la gaze / *la gaz* / – the gauze

les gouttes (f.) / *le gut* / – the drops

la médicament / le remède / *la medikamã / lə Rəmɛd* / – the medecine / the remedy

la serviette hygiénique / *la sɛRvjɛt iʒjenik* / – the pad

la pilule / *la pilyl* / – contraceptive pill

la poudre / *la pudr* / – powder

le préservatif / *lə pRezɛRvatif* / – condom

le talc / *lə talk* / – talc

le comprimé / *lə kɔ̃pRime* / – the tablet

Je voudrais quelque chose. / *ʒə vudre kelk ʃoz* / – I would like something.

    contre la toux / *kɔ̃tR la tu* / – against coughing

    contre la grippe / *kɔ̃tR la grip* / – against the flu

Ce remède n'est délivré que sur ordonnance. / *sə Rəmɛd ne delivre k syr ɔrdɔnãs* / This remedy is only available on prescription.

J'ai besoin de ce médicament. / *ʒɛ bəzwɛ̃ də sə medikamã* / – I need this medicine.

Ça se prend comment ? / *sa s pʀɑ̃d kɔmɑ̃* / – How is it taken?

C'est couvert par l'assurance ? / *sɛ kuvɛʀ par lasyrans* / – Is it covered by insurance?

Quand dois-je prendre les comprimés? / *kɑ̃ dwa ʒə pʀɑ̃dʀ le kɔ̃pʀime* / – When should I take the tablets ?

> **Deux fois par jour.** / *dø fwa par ʒuʀ* / – Two times a day.

> **Avant (après) les repas.** / *avɑ̃ / apʀɛ le repa* / – Before (after) meals.

Pour usage externe. / *pur yzaʒ ɛkstɛʀn* / – For external use.

Il faut agiter avant de s'en servir. / *il fo aʒite avɑ̃ d sɑ̃ sɛʀviʀ* / – You have to shake before using it.

Expressing Emotions

To express your feelings in French, you can use two verbs, either "*être*" or "*se sentir*", both followed by an adjective. Be aware that feminine adjectives acquire an -e, which changes how the last consonant is pronounced.

Comment te sens-tu ? / *kɔmɑ̃ t sɑ̃ ty* / – How do you feel?

Je suis / Je me sens / *ʒə sɥi / ʒə m sɑ̃* / – I am / I feel

> **fâché(e)** / *faʃe* / – angry

> **ennuyé(e)** /*enɥje* / – bored

> **honteux, honteuse** / *ɔ̃tø / ɔ̃tøz* / – ashamed

> **tranquille** / *tʀɑ̃kil* / – calm

> **gai(e)** / *ge* / cheerful

> **assuré(e)** / *asyre* / – insured

> **désorienté(e)** / *dezɔʀjɑ̃te* / – disoriented

> **ravi(e)** / *ravi* / – delighted

163

déprimé(e) / *deprime* / – depressed

épuisé(e) / *epɥize* / – exhausted

frustré(e) / *frustre* / – frustrated

heureux, heureuse / *øʀø* / *øʀøz* / – happy

horrifié(e) / *ɔʀifje* / – horrified

excité(e) / *ɛksite* / – excited

agacé(e) / *agase* / – annoyed

pressé(e) / *pʀɛse* / – in a hurry

triste / *tʀist* / – sad

effrayé(e) / *efʀeje* / – scared

content(e) / *kɔ̃tã* / – satisfied

nerveux, nerveuse / *nɛʀvø* / *nɛʀvøz* /– nervous

surpris(e) / *surprise* / – surprised

fatigué(e) / *fatige* / – tired

malheureux, malheureuse / *maløʀø* / *maløʀøz* / – unhappy

inquiet, inquiète / *ɛ̃kjɛ* / *ɛ̃kjɛt* / – worried

At the Spa

la piscine / *la pisin* / – pool

la sauna / *la sona* / – sauna

le vestiaire / *lə vɛstjɛʀ* /– locker area

le gymnase / *lə ʒimnaz* / – fitness centre

le salon de beauté / *lə salon də bote* / – beauty salon

zone d'exercices / *zon dɛgzɛʀsis* / – exercice area

la piscine d'eau salée / *la pisin do sale* / – saltwater pool

164

le banc de sauna / *lə bã də sona* /– sauna bench

le peignoir / *lə pɛɲwaʀ* / – bathrobe

le bain chaud / *lə bɛ̃ ʃo* / – hot tub

les pantoufles / *le pãtuﬂ* /– slippers

la serviette / *la sɛʀvjɛt* /– towel

le traitement / *lə tʀɛtmã* / – treatment

      de beauté / *də bote* / – beauty treatment

      pour la peau / *pur la po* / – skin treatment

      corporel / *korporel* /– body treatment

le soin / *lə swɛ̃* / – care, treatment

- **du visage** / *dy vizaʒ* / – facial treatment

- **des mains** / *de mɛ̃* / – hand treatment

- **des pieds** / *de pje* / – foot treatment

la manicure / *lə manikyr* / – manicure

la pédicure / *lə pedikyr* / – pedicure

le soin des ongles / *lə swɛ̃* / – nail care

l'aromathérapie / *laʀɔmateʀapi* /– aromatherapy

épilation / *lepilasjɔ̃* /– waxing, depilation

le contour des sourcils / *kɔ̃tuʀ de sursi* / – eyebrow threading

le bain turc / *lə bɛ̃ tyrk* / – steam bath

le massage suédois / *lə masaʒ syedwa* / – Swedish massage

le massage sportif / *lə masaʒ spɔrtif* /– sport massage

le massage aux pierres chaudes / *lə masaʒ o pjɛʀə ʃod* / – hot stone massage

Pouvez-vous me dire où est le jacuzzi ? / *puve vu mə dir u e lə ʒakyzi* / – Can you tell me where the jacuzzi is?

La piscine est-elle chauffée ? / *la pisin et el ʃofe* / – Is the swimming pool heated?

Y a-t-il un endroit pour s'allonger ? / *jatil œ□ □□d□wa pur sal□□□e* / – Is there somewhere to lie down?

Proposez-vous des soins pour le corps ? / *propoze vu de swɛ̃ pur lə kor* / – Do you offer body treatments?

Est-ce que la piscine extérieure est ouverte pendant le printemps ? / *esk la pisin □kste□jœ□ et uvɛʀt pãdã lə pʀɛ̃tã* / – Is the outdoor pool open in the spring?

Proposez-vous / *propoze vu* / – Do you offer

> **des soins à la pierre chaude ?** / de *swɛ̃ a la pjɛʀ ʃod* / – hot stone treatments?

> **épilation ?** / epilasjɔ̃ / – waxing

Peut-on faire un massage à deux ? / *pø □□ f□□ œ□ masa□ a dø* / – Is it possible to have a massage for two?

Où sont les vestiaires pour femmes/hommes ? / *u son le vɛstjɛʀ pur fam/ɔm* ?/ – Where can I find dressing rooms for women/men?

Chapter 17: Telephone and Internet

La chose la plus importante en communication, c'est d'entendre ce qui n'est pas dit.

Peter Drucker

During a stay in France, you can benefit from the WiFi of the hotel in which you are staying, and certain public places (such as train stations and cafes). However, many tourists choose to buy a French SIM card to have internet access at all times.

The main French operators **Orange** or **SFR** offer a prepaid card without any strings attached. The package is adapted for tourists, offering 2 hours of calls in France and Europe, unlimited SMS/MMS, and a certain amount of internet in France and Europe for 14 days.

You can find the SIM card at Orange shops, tobacco stores, petrol stations, supermarkets, and at the airport. There are five languages in the accompanying booklet, so you can use it as a guide to install the card.

Telephone

le portable / *lə portabl* / – the mobile phone

la carte prépayée / *la kart prepeje* / – the prepaid card

la batterie de portable / *la batri də portabl* / – the mobile battery

le chargeur de batterie / *ʃaʀʒœʀ də batri* / – the battery charger

la ligne fixe / *la liɲ fiks* / – the fixed line

Est-ce que je peux utiliser votre téléphone ? / ɛsk ʒə pø utilize votr telefon / – Can I use your phone?

Allô. Oui /alo/ wi / – – Hello. Yes.

On vous appellera au téléphone ! / ɔ̃ vuzapəlera o telefon / – We'll call you on the phone !

Pouvez-vous répéter s'il vous plaît. / puve vu repete sil vu plɛ / – Could you repeat please?

Excusez-moi, j'ai dû me tromper de numéro. / ekskuze mwa ʒɛ dy mə trompe də numero / – Sorry, I must have gotten the number wrong.

Je vous entends mal. / ʒə vuzɑ̃tɑ̃d mal / – I can barely hear you.

Vous pouvez me le/la passer ? / vu puve m lə / la pase / – Can you pass me (person's name)?

À qui voulez-vous parler ? / a ki vule vu parle / – Who would you like to speak to?

J'aimerais parler avec ( ) / ʒemre parle avɛk / – I would like to speak with ( ).

La ligne est toujours occupée. / la liɲ e tuʒuʀ ɔkype / – The line is always busy.

Est-ce que je peux laisser un message ? / ☐sk ☐☐ pø lese œ☐ mesa☐ / – Can I leave a message?

Essayez de téléphoner dans une heure ? / eseje də telef☐ne d☐☐ yn œ☐ / – Try to call in an hour?

La batterie est presque déchargée. / la batri e presk deʃaʀʒe / – The battery is almost empty.

Il me faut recharger le crédit. / il m fo ʀəʃaʀʒe lə kredi / – I need to top up the credit.

Quel est le numéro pour appeler la police / une ambulance ?
/ *kɛl e lə numero pur apple la polis/ yn ãbylãs* / – What is the number to call the police / an ambulance?

Getting a Mobile Card

la carte sim / *la kart sim* / – to buy a sim card

    prépayée / *prepeje* / – prepaid

une recharge mobile / *yn ʀəʃaʀʒ mobil* / – a mobile recharge

le bureau de tabac / *lə buro də taba* / – the tobacco shop

les boutiques des opérateurs / *le butik dez□pe□atœ□* / – operators shops

le forfait / *lə fɔʀfɛ* / – the package

    sans abonnement/engagement / *sanzabɔnmã* / *ãgaʒmã* / without subscription

Où puis-je acheter une carte SIM ? / *u pɥi ʒə aʃəte yn kart sim* / – Where can I buy a SIM card?

Je voudrais acheter une carte SIM pour 14 jours. / *ʒə vudre aʃəte yn kart sim pur katɔʀz ʒuʀ* / – I would like to buy a Sim card for 14 days.

Quel est le prix d'une carte SIM pour une durée d'un mois ? / *k□l e l□ pri dyn kart sim pur yn dyre dœ□ mwa* / – What is the price of a monthly SIM card?

Est-ce qu'il est possible d'acheter une carte Sim en ligne ? / *ɛskil e posibl daʃəte yn kart sim ã liɲ* / – Is it possible to buy a sim card online?

Qu'est-ce qui est inclus dans le forfait ? / *kɛskil e ɛ̃kly dã lə fɔʀfɛ* / – What is included in the package?

Est-ce qu'on reçoit des appels illimités ? / *ɛskɔ̃ ʀəswa dezapɛl ilimite* / – Do we receive unlimited calls?

Est-ce que je peux acheter la carte sans abonnement ? / ɛsk ʒə pø aʃəte la kart sãnz abɔnmã / – Is it possible to buy the sim card without subscription?

Combien d'appels on obtient avec cette carte SIM ? / kɔ̃bjɛ̃ dapɛl ɔ̃ ɔptjɛ̃ avɛk sɛt kart sim /– How many calls do we get with this SIM card?

Les appels vers l'étranger sont–ils inclus dans le prix ? / lezapɛl vɛʁ letʁãʒe sɔ̃til ɛ̃kly dã lə pri /– Are calls abroad included in the price?

Combien d'internet est inclus dans le prix ? / kɔ̃bjɛ̃ dɛ̃tɛʁnɛt e ɛ̃kly dã lə pri /– How much internet is included in the price?

Qu'est ce qui se passe si je dépasse cette limite ? / kɛski sə pas si ʒə depas sɛt limit / – What happens if I exceed this limit?

Comment je peux recharger le crédit ? / kɔmã ʒə pø ʁəʃaʁʒe lə kredi / – How do I top up the credit?

Quel est le prix des recharges pour une durée de 6 jours ? / kɛl e lə pri de ʁəʃaʁʒ pur yn dyre də si ʒuʁ / – How much is the price for a6 day top up?

Internet

se connecter sur Internet / se brancher sur le Net / s kɔnɛkte syr ɛ̃tɛʁnɛt/ s bʁãʃe syr lə net / – to connect to the internet

la connexion / la kɔnɛksjɔ̃ / – the connection

    lente / lãt /– slow

    rapide / rapid / – fast

le réseau / lə rezo / – the network

le mot de passe / lə mot de pas / – password

afficher le mot de passe / afiʃe lə mo d pas / – to show the password

se connecter au réseau Wi-Fi / *s kɔnɛkte o rezo wifi* / – to connect to the Wi-Fi network

acceder à internet / *aksede a ɛ̃tɛʀnɛt* / – to access the internet

@ arobase / *arobaz* / – at sign

– tiret / *tire* / – hyphen

le lien / *lə ljɛ̃* / – the link

le site Web / *lə sit vɛb* / – the website

le courrier électronique / *lə kuʀje elɛktʀɔnik* / – e–mail

répondre à ses mails / *repondr a se mɛl* / – answer his emails

joindre un fichier / □w□□d□ œ□ *fi*□*je* / – to attach a file

enregistrer / *ɑ̃ʀəʒistʀe* / – to save, to record

les réseaux sociaux / *le rezo sɔsjo* / – social media

Avez-vous une connexion Internet ? / *ave vu yn kɔnɛksjɔ̃ ɛ̃tɛʀnɛt* / – Do you have internet access?

Y-a-t-il une connexion Internet gratuite à proximité ? / *jatil yn kɔnɛksjɔ̃ gʀatɥit a pʀɔksimite* / – Is there free internet nearby?

Qu'est-ce qu'un mot de passe Internet ? / *kesk œ□ mo d□ pas ɛ̃tɛʀnɛt* / – What is the internet password?

Je n'arrive pas à me connecter à l'internet. / *ʒə nariv pa a mə kɔnɛkte alɛ̃tɛʀnɛt* / – I can't connect to the internet.

Pourriez-vous partager votre internet ? / *purje vu paʀtaʒe votr ɛ̃tɛʀnɛt* / – Could you share your internet?

Computer

l'écran / *lekʀɑ̃* /– screen

le clavier / *lə klavje* / – keyboard

la touche / *la tuʃ* / – key

    appuyer sur une touche / *apyije syr yn tuʃ* / – to press a key

allumer l'ordinateur / *alyme l□□dinatœ□* / – to start the computer

éteindre l'ordinateur / *et□□d□ l□□dinatœ□* / – to shut down the computer

cliquer sur / *klikɛ syr* / – to click on

doublecliquer sur / *dubl klikɛ syr* / – to double–click on

copiercoller / *kopije kole* / – to copy and paste

Documents and emails

ouvrir / *uvʀiʀ* / – to open

    le fichier / *lə fiʃje* / – the file

    le document / *lə dɔkymɑ̃* / – the document

    le programme / *lə pʀɔgʀam* /– the program

créer un fichier / *k□ee œ□ fi□je* / – to create a document

fermer un fichier / *f□□me œ□ fi□je* / – to close a document

sélectionner un fichier / *sel□ksj□ne œ□ fi□je* / – to select a document

télécharger un fichier / *teleʃaʀʒe œ□ fi□je* / – to download a file

sauvegarder un document / *sovgaʀde dɔkymɑ̃* / – to save a document

effacer un document / *efase dɔkymɑ̃* / – to erase a document

imprimer un document / *ɛ̃pʁime dɔkymɑ̃* /– to print a document

l'imprimante / *lɛ̃pʁimɑ̃t* / – printer

Quelle est ton adresse e-mail ? / *kɛl e ton adres imel* / – What is your email adress?

Je vous envoie ci-joint le fichier. / *ʒə vuzɑ̃vwa si ʒwɛ̃ lə fiʃje* / – I am sending you a file attached.

Je dois chercher quelque chose sur internet. / *ʒə dwa ʃɛʁʃe kɛlkʃoz syr ɛ̃tɛʁnɛt* / – I have to look something up on the internet.

Je clique sur l'icône mais le document ne s'affiche pas. / *ʒə klik syr likon mɛ lə dɔkymɑ̃ nə safiʃ pa* / – I click on the icon but the document doesn't appear.

Est-ce que vous pouvez imprimer en deux exemplaires ? / *esk vu puve ɛ̃pʁime ɑ̃ dø ɛgzɑ̃plɛʁ* / – Can you print two copies?

Mon ordinateur ne démarre pas. / *mo □□dinatœ□ n□ dema□e pa* / – My computer is not starting.

Où puis-je faire réparer mon ordinateur portable ? / *u p□i □□ f□□ repare m□□ □□dinatœ□ portabl* / – Where can I get my laptop fixed?

Chapter 18: Emergencies

La simplification de la vie est l'une des étapes de la paix intérieure.

Milred Norman

Travelers to France, or to any country, should know their emergency numbers in case of an emergency. For French Emergency Medical Assistance, you'll need to call 15. For emergency police number, call 17, for fire brigade call 18. There's also a general Emergency number that's valid for the whole of Europe **112**.

Urgences

Au secours ! / *o səkuʀ* / – Help!

Au feu ! / *o fø* / – Fire !

Au voleur ! / *o v☐lœ☐* / – Thief !

Attention ! / *atãsjɔ̃* / – Attention !

Pouvez-vous m'aider / nous aider. / *puve vu mede / nuzede* / – Can you help me/us.

C'est très urgent. / *sɛ trezyʀʒã* / – This is very urgent.

Où est l'hôpital le plus proche ? / *u e lɔpital lə ply pʀɔʃ* / – Where is the nearest hospital?

Appelez la police / une ambulance. / *apele la polis / yn ãbylãs* / – Call the police / an ambulance.

Notre chambre a été cambriolée. / *notr ʃãbʀ a ete kãbʀijɔle* / – Our room was broken into.

Je n'ai pas d'argent. / ʒə nɛ pa daʀʒã / – I don't have money.

J'ai eu un accident. / ʒ□ y œ□ aksid□□ / – I had an accident.

Quelqu'un a volé mon passeport. / k□lkœ□ a vole mo p□sp□□ / – Someone stole my passport.

Ma valise est perdue. / ma valiz e perdy / – My suitcase is lost.

J'ai besoin de prendre mes médicaments. / ʒɛ bəzwɛ̃ də pʀãdʀ me medikamã / I need to take my medication.

Jai mal. / ʒɛ mal / – I am in pain.

Je n'ai pas d'assurance voyage. / ʒ nɛ pa dasyʀãs vwajaʒ / – I don't have travel insurance.

Mon portable est déchargé. / mɔ̃ portabl e deʃaʀʒe / – My phone is dead.

Je peux passer un coup de fil chez vous ? / ʒə pø pase œ□ ku d fil □e vu / – Can I make a phone call from your house?

Où sont les toilettes ? / u sɔ̃ le twalɛt / – Where is the toilet?

J'ai perdu les clés (de la voiture) . / ʒɛ perdy le kle / – I've lost the keys (from the car)

J'ai besoin de passer un coup de fil. / ʒɛ b□zw□□ d pase œ□ ku d□ fil / – I need to make a phone call.

Je me suis perdu. / ʒə m sɥi perdy / – I got lost.

Je ne sais pas comment ça marche. / ʒə n sɛ pa kɔmã sa maʀʃ / – I don't know how it works.

Vous pouvez me le prêter ? / vu puve m lə pʀete / – Could you lend it to me?

On peut passer la nuit ici ? / ɔ̃ pø pase la nɥi isi / – Can we spend the night here?

Je m'adresse à qui ? / ʒə m adʀɛs a ki / – Who am I talking to?

Je ne vous comprends pas. / *ʒə n vu kɔ̃prãd pa* / – I don't understand you.

Je veux un interprète. / □□ *vø œ*□ □□*t*□□*p*□□*t* / – I want an interpreter.

Police

Où est le poste de police le plus proche ? / *u e lə post d polis lə ply prɔʃ* / – Where is the nearest police station?

Je voudrais signaler le vol / la perte / une attaque / un enlèvement. / *ʒə vudrɛ siɲale lə vol / la pɛrt / yn atak / œ*□ *ãlɛvmã* / – I would like to report the theft / the loss / an attack / a kidnapping.

Je n'ai pas de pièce d'identité sur moi. / *ʒə nɛ pa də pjɛs didãtite syr mwa* / – I don't have any ID on me.

J'ai été attaqué. / *ʒete atake* / – I was attacked.

Ils étaient armés d'un pistolet/couteau. / *ilzet*□ *arme dœ*□ *pist*□*l*□ / *kuto* / – They were armed with a gun/knife.

J'ai été violé. / *ʒɛ ete vjɔle* / – I've been raped.

Un homme me harcèle. / *œ*□ *ɔm mə arsəl* / – A man is harassing me.

J'ai besoin d'aide. / *ʒɛ bəzwɛ̃ dɛd* / – I need help.

J'ai été témoin d'un accident. / *ʒɛ ete temw*□□ *dœ*□ *aksid*□□ / I witnessed an accident.

Je veux déposer une plainte. / *ʒə vø depozer yn plɛ̃t* / – I want to file a complaint.

Je voudrais parler à mon avocat. / *ʒə vudre parle a mɔ̃ avɔka* / – I would like to speak to my lawyer.

Pourquoi je suis arrêté ? / *purkwa ʒə sɥi arete* / – Why am I arrested?

Pourquoi vous m'accusez ? / *puʀkwa vu makuze* / – Why are you accusing me?

Je ne connais pas cette personne. / *ʒə n konɛ pa sɛt person* / – I don't know this person.

Je n'ai pas consommé d'alcool. / *ʒə nɛ pa kɔ̃sɔme de lalkol* / – I did not consume alcohol.

J'ai droit à un appel téléphonique. / □□ *drwa a œ□ apɛl telefɔnik* / I have the right to a phone call.

Je vais déposer une plainte. / *ʒə vɛ depoze yn plɛ̃t* / I am going to file a complaint.

Car Issues

Vous pouvez appeler quelqu'un pour me remorquer ? / *vu puve apele k□lkœ□ pur m ʀəmɔʀke* / – Can you call someone to tow me?

Quel est le numéro du service de dépannage ? / *kɛl e lə numero dy servis də depanaʒ* / – What is the breakdown service number?

Je suis sur la route ( ), environ à ( ) kilomètres de la ville. / *ʒə sɥi syr la rut, ɑ̃viʀɔ̃ a kilɔmɛtʀ də la vil* / – I am on route ( ), about ( ) km from town.

Où est le garage le plus proche ? / *u e lə gaʀaʒ lə ply pʀɔʃ* / – Where is the nearest garage?

Vous pouvez me remorquer à la ville la plus proche / au garage le plus proche ? / *vu puve m ʀəmɔʀke a la vil la ply pʀɔʃ / o gaʀaʒ lə ply pʀɔʃ* / Can you tow me to the nearest town / nearest garage?

Ça va couter combien ? / *sa va kute kɔ̃bjɛ̃* / – How much will it cost?

Vous pouvez m'emmener en ville ? / *vu puve mɑ̃məne ɑ̃ vil* / – Can you take me to town?

Est-ce que je peux louer une autre voiture près d'ici ? / *esk ʒə pø lwe yn otr vwatyʀ predisi* / – Can I rent another car near here ?

Ma voiture a été enlevée. / *ma vwatyr a ete ãləve* /– My car has been taken away.

On a eu un accident. / *ɔ̃ a y œ□ aksid□□* / – We had an accident.

Nous avons un blessé ici. / *nuzavon œ□ blese isi* / – We have an injured here.

Ma voiture est sortie de la route. / *ma vwatyr e sorti də la rut* /– My car went off the road.

La priorité était à moi. / *la pʀijɔʀite ete a mwa* /– The priority was mine.

J'ai fermé la voiture avec les clés dedans. / *ʒɛ ferme la vwatyr avɛk le kle dədã* / – I locked the car with the keys inside.

On est resté bloqué dans un embouteillage. / *□□ e reste bl□ke d□□ œ□ □□but□ja□* / – We got stuck in a traffic jam.

J'ai crevé. / *ʒɛ kreve*/ – I got a flat tire.

Mes freins ont lâché. / *me fʀɛ̃ ɔ̃ laʃe* / – My brakes gave out.

Le conducteur qui a causé l'accident s'est enfui. / *lə k□□dyktœ□ ki a koze laksid□□ se □□ʃ□i□* / – The driver who caused the accident escaped.

J'ai un problème avec ma voiture. / *ʒɛ œ□ p□□bl□m av□k ma vwatyr* / – I have a problem with my car.

Je suis en panne d'essence. / *ʒə sɥi ã pan desãs* / – I am out of gas.

Conclusion

Everyone tells you that speaking a language is not a one-day task, and above all that it requires discipline, consistency and hard work. They assure you there's no way to be a fluent French speaker in a short period of time. Well, maybe you don't have to be fluent to deal with everyday situations in French.

Having a handbook at your fingertips is not only a great shortcut to handling all possible situations when traveling to France, but also a great starting point for anyone looking to learn French. Being exposed to all kinds of everyday sentences and vocabulary helps you become sensitive to French language patterns and be able to create sentences of your own, which is the end goal of every language learner.

Our goal was to create a book that would cover all possible situations that may arise when traveling to France. The book is structured into logical sequences that correspond to actual contextual situations. We carefully covered all possible situations you may encounter as a foreigner traveling around France, assembling the most important words and phrases in logical format. 15 topics cover the 15 most frequent everyday situations, from traveling, transportation, ordering at the restaurant, grocery shopping, going to nature, sightseeing, weather, visiting a doctor, and much more, allowing you to build your vocabulary in different areas.

However, this book does more than just prepare you to get by in all possible situations. It is designed for students who want to learn elementary grammar and see how nouns, articles, adjectives, and verbs behave in French. The first three chapters are created with common beginner's troubles in mind, such as understanding pronunciation, learning elementary grammar, and basic vocabulary.

You already noted that certain structures, such as "I am", and "where is" appeared frequently throughout the book. After practicing the essential structures included here, you can recall the statements easier and even create your phrases.

We begin by focusing on greetings and civilities, then move on to meeting people and expressing time, followed by weather conditions. Having learned how to keep small talk like a French person in Paris, you head off to learn more about traveling and sightseeing in the upcoming chapter, where you get useful directions about traveling in both urban and rural areas. As you read chapter nine, you find yourself looking for a hotel room, going through the steps of booking, arriving, paying, expressing your complaints, etc. Chapter ten is about attending cultural events and entertainment. Section eleven on transportation is particularly important, since moving around is unavoidable when you are traveling.

The twelfth chapter helps you order food in a restaurant or go grocery shopping. Next, you learn about money, such as paying, going to the bank or exchanging money, even using Apple pay to process payment. Following chapters help you handle situations such as job search, going to the doctor, dentist, or pharmacy. Next, you'll get useful information about purchasing a tourist sim card with the internet, followed by essential phrases related to telephone, internet, computer or documents. At the end, the final chapter helps you solve emergency situations and potential issues.

It may surprise you to learn that you don't need to know a lot of French or complete grammar to interact with locals. Typically, people use a limited number of words and expressions in a single situation. The goal was to create a book that would reconcile your need to learn grammar with the need to cope with everyday situations in French in an easy and practical way. By accompanying the context–based vocabulary and sentences with grammar notes, we aimed to get the maximum benefit from this book.

With 15 different topics under your belt and a solid foundation in French grammar, you are well prepared to speak French, even with natives.

It gives you the freedom to get through all the most common situations, such as ordering at a restaurant, going through passport control, finding accommodation, purchasing tickets, printing documents, exchanging money, going to the doctor's office, solving computer or internet issues, and much more.

Now you just need to be brave and apply what you've learned.

Made in the USA
Las Vegas, NV
30 November 2024

13034603R10111